Microsoft®
Training & Certification

2011A: Troubleshooting Microsoft® Exchange Server 2003

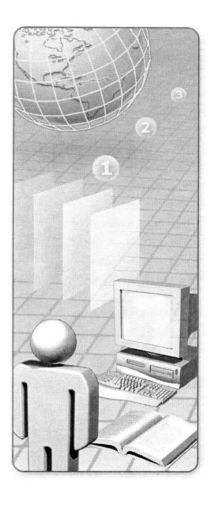

Microsoft®

Workshop: 2011A
Part Number: X10-27588
Released: 12/2003

END-USER LICENSE AGREEMENT FOR MICROSOFT OFFICIAL CURRICULUM COURSEWARE –STUDENT EDITION

PLEASE READ THIS END-USER LICENSE AGREEMENT ("EULA") CAREFULLY. BY USING THE MATERIALS AND/OR USING OR INSTALLING THE SOFTWARE THAT ACCOMPANIES THIS EULA (COLLECTIVELY, THE "LICENSED CONTENT"), YOU AGREE TO THE TERMS OF THIS EULA. IF YOU DO NOT AGREE, DO NOT USE THE LICENSED CONTENT.

1.   **GENERAL.** This EULA is a legal agreement between you (either an individual or a single entity) and Microsoft Corporation ("Microsoft"). This EULA governs the Licensed Content, which includes computer software (including online and electronic documentation), training materials, and any other associated media and printed materials. This EULA applies to updates, supplements, add-on components, and Internet-based services components of the Licensed Content that Microsoft may provide or make available to you unless Microsoft provides other terms with the update, supplement, add-on component, or Internet-based services component. Microsoft reserves the right to discontinue any Internet-based services provided to you or made available to you through the use of the Licensed Content. This EULA also governs any product support services relating to the Licensed Content except as may be included in another agreement between you and Microsoft. An amendment or addendum to this EULA may accompany the Licensed Content.

2.   **GENERAL GRANT OF LICENSE.** Microsoft grants you the following rights, conditioned on your compliance with all the terms and conditions of this EULA. Microsoft grants you a limited, non-exclusive, royalty-free license to install and use the Licensed Content solely in conjunction with your participation as a student in an Authorized Training Session (as defined below). You may install and use one copy of the software on a single computer, device, workstation, terminal, or other digital electronic or analog device ("Device"). You may make a second copy of the software and install it on a portable Device for the exclusive use of the person who is the primary user of the first copy of the software. A license for the software may not be shared for use by multiple end users. An "Authorized Training Session" means a training session conducted at a Microsoft Certified Technical Education Center, an IT Academy, via a Microsoft Certified Partner, or such other entity as Microsoft may designate from time to time in writing, by a Microsoft Certified Trainer (for more information on these entities, please visit www.microsoft.com). WITHOUT LIMITING THE FOREGOING, COPYING OR REPRODUCTION OF THE LICENSED CONTENT TO ANY SERVER OR LOCATION FOR FURTHER REPRODUCTION OR REDISTRIBUTION IS EXPRESSLY PROHIBITED.

3.   **DESCRIPTION OF OTHER RIGHTS AND LICENSE LIMITATIONS**

    3.1   *Use of Documentation and Printed Training Materials.*

        3.1.1   The documents and related graphics included in the Licensed Content may include technical inaccuracies or typographical errors. Changes are periodically made to the content. Microsoft may make improvements and/or changes in any of the components of the Licensed Content at any time without notice. The names of companies, products, people, characters and/or data mentioned in the Licensed Content may be fictitious and are in no way intended to represent any real individual, company, product or event, unless otherwise noted.

        3.1.2   Microsoft grants you the right to reproduce portions of documents (such as student workbooks, white papers, press releases, datasheets and FAQs) (the "Documents") provided with the Licensed Content. You may not print any book (either electronic or print version) in its entirety. If you choose to reproduce Documents, you agree that: (a) use of such printed Documents will be solely in conjunction with your personal training use; (b) the Documents will not republished or posted on any network computer or broadcast in any media; (c) any reproduction will include either the Document's original copyright notice or a copyright notice to Microsoft's benefit substantially in the format provided below; and (d) to comply with all terms and conditions of this EULA. In addition, no modifications may made to any Document.

        Form of Notice:

        © 2003. Reprinted with permission by Microsoft Corporation. All rights reserved.

        Microsoft and Windows are either registered trademarks or trademarks of Microsoft Corporation in the US and/or other countries. Other product and company names mentioned herein may be the trademarks of their respective owners.

    3.2   *Use of Media Elements.* The Licensed Content may include certain photographs, clip art, animations, sounds, music, and video clips (together "Media Elements"). You may not modify these Media Elements.

    3.3   *Use of Sample Code.* In the event that the Licensed Content includes sample code in source or object format ("Sample Code"), Microsoft grants you a limited, non-exclusive, royalty-free license to use, copy and modify the Sample Code; if you elect to exercise the foregoing rights, you agree to comply with all other terms and conditions of this EULA, including without limitation Sections 3.4, 3.5, and 6.

    3.4   *Permitted Modifications.* In the event that you exercise any rights provided under this EULA to create modifications of the Licensed Content, you agree that any such modifications: (a) will not be used for providing training where a fee is charged in public or private classes; (b) indemnify, hold harmless, and defend Microsoft from and against any claims or lawsuits, including attorneys' fees, which arise from or result from your use of any modified version of the Licensed Content; and (c) not to transfer or assign any rights to any modified version of the Licensed Content to any third party without the express written permission of Microsoft.

3.5   *Reproduction/Redistribution Licensed Content.* Except as expressly provided in this EULA, you may not reproduce or distribute the Licensed Content or any portion thereof (including any permitted modifications) to any third parties without the express written permission of Microsoft.

4.   **RESERVATION OF RIGHTS AND OWNERSHIP.** Microsoft reserves all rights not expressly granted to you in this EULA. The Licensed Content is protected by copyright and other intellectual property laws and treaties. Microsoft or its suppliers own the title, copyright, and other intellectual property rights in the Licensed Content. You may not remove or obscure any copyright, trademark or patent notices that appear on the Licensed Content, or any components thereof, as delivered to you. **The Licensed Content is licensed, not sold.**

5.   **LIMITATIONS ON REVERSE ENGINEERING, DECOMPILATION, AND DISASSEMBLY.** You may not reverse engineer, decompile, or disassemble the Software or Media Elements, except and only to the extent that such activity is expressly permitted by applicable law notwithstanding this limitation.

6.   **LIMITATIONS ON SALE, RENTAL, ETC. AND CERTAIN ASSIGNMENTS.** You may not provide commercial hosting services with, sell, rent, lease, lend, sublicense, or assign copies of the Licensed Content, or any portion thereof (including any permitted modifications thereof) on a stand-alone basis or as part of any collection, product or service.

7.   **CONSENT TO USE OF DATA.** You agree that Microsoft and its affiliates may collect and use technical information gathered as part of the product support services provided to you, if any, related to the Licensed Content. Microsoft may use this information solely to improve our products or to provide customized services or technologies to you and will not disclose this information in a form that personally identifies you.

8.   **LINKS TO THIRD PARTY SITES.** You may link to third party sites through the use of the Licensed Content. The third party sites are not under the control of Microsoft, and Microsoft is not responsible for the contents of any third party sites, any links contained in third party sites, or any changes or updates to third party sites. Microsoft is not responsible for webcasting or any other form of transmission received from any third party sites. Microsoft is providing these links to third party sites to you only as a convenience, and the inclusion of any link does not imply an endorsement by Microsoft of the third party site.

9.   **ADDITIONAL LICENSED CONTENT/SERVICES.** This EULA applies to updates, supplements, add-on components, or Internet-based services components, of the Licensed Content that Microsoft may provide to you or make available to you after the date you obtain your initial copy of the Licensed Content, unless we provide other terms along with the update, supplement, add-on component, or Internet-based services component. Microsoft reserves the right to discontinue any Internet-based services provided to you or made available to you through the use of the Licensed Content.

10.   **U.S. GOVERNMENT LICENSE RIGHTS**. All software provided to the U.S. Government pursuant to solicitations issued on or after December 1, 1995 is provided with the commercial license rights and restrictions described elsewhere herein. All software provided to the U.S. Government pursuant to solicitations issued prior to December 1, 1995 is provided with "Restricted Rights" as provided for in FAR, 48 CFR 52.227-14 (JUNE 1987) or DFAR, 48 CFR 252.227-7013 (OCT 1988), as applicable.

11.   **EXPORT RESTRICTIONS**. You acknowledge that the Licensed Content is subject to U.S. export jurisdiction. You agree to comply with all applicable international and national laws that apply to the Licensed Content, including the U.S. Export Administration Regulations, as well as end-user, end-use, and destination restrictions issued by U.S. and other governments. For additional information see <http://www.microsoft.com/exporting/>.

12.   **TRANSFER.** The initial user of the Licensed Content may make a one-time permanent transfer of this EULA and Licensed Content to another end user, provided the initial user retains no copies of the Licensed Content. The transfer may not be an indirect transfer, such as a consignment. Prior to the transfer, the end user receiving the Licensed Content must agree to all the EULA terms.

13.   **"NOT FOR RESALE" LICENSED CONTENT.** Licensed Content identified as "Not For Resale" or "NFR," may not be sold or otherwise transferred for value, or used for any purpose other than demonstration, test or evaluation.

14.   **TERMINATION.** Without prejudice to any other rights, Microsoft may terminate this EULA if you fail to comply with the terms and conditions of this EULA. In such event, you must destroy all copies of the Licensed Content and all of its component parts.

15.   **DISCLAIMER OF WARRANTIES. TO THE MAXIMUM EXTENT PERMITTED BY APPLICABLE LAW, MICROSOFT AND ITS SUPPLIERS PROVIDE THE LICENSED CONTENT AND SUPPORT SERVICES (IF ANY) *AS IS AND WITH ALL FAULTS*, AND MICROSOFT AND ITS SUPPLIERS HEREBY DISCLAIM ALL OTHER WARRANTIES AND CONDITIONS, WHETHER EXPRESS, IMPLIED OR STATUTORY, INCLUDING, BUT NOT LIMITED TO, ANY (IF ANY) IMPLIED WARRANTIES, DUTIES OR CONDITIONS OF MERCHANTABILITY, OF FITNESS FOR A PARTICULAR PURPOSE, OF RELIABILITY OR AVAILABILITY, OF ACCURACY OR COMPLETENESS OF RESPONSES, OF RESULTS, OF WORKMANLIKE EFFORT, OF LACK OF VIRUSES, AND OF LACK OF NEGLIGENCE, ALL WITH REGARD TO THE LICENSED CONTENT, AND THE PROVISION OF OR FAILURE TO PROVIDE SUPPORT OR OTHER SERVICES, INFORMATION, SOFTWARE, AND RELATED CONTENT THROUGH THE LICENSED CONTENT, OR OTHERWISE ARISING OUT OF THE USE OF THE LICENSED CONTENT. ALSO, THERE IS NO WARRANTY OR CONDITION OF TITLE, QUIET ENJOYMENT, QUIET POSSESSION, CORRESPONDENCE TO DESCRIPTION OR NON-INFRINGEMENT WITH REGARD TO THE LICENSED CONTENT. THE ENTIRE RISK AS TO THE QUALITY, OR ARISING OUT OF THE USE OR PERFORMANCE OF THE LICENSED CONTENT, AND ANY SUPPORT SERVICES, REMAINS WITH YOU.**

16.   **EXCLUSION OF INCIDENTAL, CONSEQUENTIAL AND CERTAIN OTHER DAMAGES. TO THE MAXIMUM EXTENT PERMITTED BY APPLICABLE LAW, IN NO EVENT SHALL MICROSOFT OR ITS SUPPLIERS BE LIABLE FOR ANY SPECIAL, INCIDENTAL, PUNITIVE, INDIRECT, OR CONSEQUENTIAL DAMAGES WHATSOEVER (INCLUDING, BUT NOT**

LIMITED TO, DAMAGES FOR LOSS OF PROFITS OR CONFIDENTIAL OR OTHER INFORMATION, FOR BUSINESS INTERRUPTION, FOR PERSONAL INJURY, FOR LOSS OF PRIVACY, FOR FAILURE TO MEET ANY DUTY INCLUDING OF GOOD FAITH OR OF REASONABLE CARE, FOR NEGLIGENCE, AND FOR ANY OTHER PECUNIARY OR OTHER LOSS WHATSOEVER) ARISING OUT OF OR IN ANY WAY RELATED TO THE USE OF OR INABILITY TO USE THE LICENSED CONTENT, THE PROVISION OF OR FAILURE TO PROVIDE SUPPORT OR OTHER SERVICES, INFORMATION, SOFTWARE, AND RELATED CONTENT THROUGH THE LICENSED CONTENT, OR OTHERWISE ARISING OUT OF THE USE OF THE LICENSED CONTENT, OR OTHERWISE UNDER OR IN CONNECTION WITH ANY PROVISION OF THIS EULA, EVEN IN THE EVENT OF THE FAULT, TORT (INCLUDING NEGLIGENCE), MISREPRESENTATION, STRICT LIABILITY, BREACH OF CONTRACT OR BREACH OF WARRANTY OF MICROSOFT OR ANY SUPPLIER, AND EVEN IF MICROSOFT OR ANY SUPPLIER HAS BEEN ADVISED OF THE POSSIBILITY OF SUCH DAMAGES. BECAUSE SOME STATES/JURISDICTIONS DO NOT ALLOW THE EXCLUSION OR LIMITATION OF LIABILITY FOR CONSEQUENTIAL OR INCIDENTAL DAMAGES, THE ABOVE LIMITATION MAY NOT APPLY TO YOU.

17. <u>LIMITATION OF LIABILITY AND REMEDIES.</u> NOTWITHSTANDING ANY DAMAGES THAT YOU MIGHT INCUR FOR ANY REASON WHATSOEVER (INCLUDING, WITHOUT LIMITATION, ALL DAMAGES REFERENCED HEREIN AND ALL DIRECT OR GENERAL DAMAGES IN CONTRACT OR ANYTHING ELSE), THE ENTIRE LIABILITY OF MICROSOFT AND ANY OF ITS SUPPLIERS UNDER ANY PROVISION OF THIS EULA AND YOUR EXCLUSIVE REMEDY HEREUNDER SHALL BE LIMITED TO THE GREATER OF THE ACTUAL DAMAGES YOU INCUR IN REASONABLE RELIANCE ON THE LICENSED CONTENT UP TO THE AMOUNT ACTUALLY PAID BY YOU FOR THE LICENSED CONTENT OR US$5.00. THE FOREGOING LIMITATIONS, EXCLUSIONS AND DISCLAIMERS SHALL APPLY TO THE MAXIMUM EXTENT PERMITTED BY APPLICABLE LAW, EVEN IF ANY REMEDY FAILS ITS ESSENTIAL PURPOSE.

18. **APPLICABLE LAW.** If you acquired this Licensed Content in the United States, this EULA is governed by the laws of the State of Washington. If you acquired this Licensed Content in Canada, unless expressly prohibited by local law, this EULA is governed by the laws in force in the Province of Ontario, Canada; and, in respect of any dispute which may arise hereunder, you consent to the jurisdiction of the federal and provincial courts sitting in Toronto, Ontario. If you acquired this Licensed Content in the European Union, Iceland, Norway, or Switzerland, then local law applies. If you acquired this Licensed Content in any other country, then local law may apply.

19. **ENTIRE AGREEMENT; SEVERABILITY.** This EULA (including any addendum or amendment to this EULA which is included with the Licensed Content) are the entire agreement between you and Microsoft relating to the Licensed Content and the support services (if any) and they supersede all prior or contemporaneous oral or written communications, proposals and representations with respect to the Licensed Content or any other subject matter covered by this EULA. To the extent the terms of any Microsoft policies or programs for support services conflict with the terms of this EULA, the terms of this EULA shall control. If any provision of this EULA is held to be void, invalid, unenforceable or illegal, the other provisions shall continue in full force and effect.

Should you have any questions concerning this EULA, or if you desire to contact Microsoft for any reason, please use the address information enclosed in this Licensed Content to contact the Microsoft subsidiary serving your country or visit Microsoft on the World Wide Web at http://www.microsoft.com.

Si vous avez acquis votre Contenu Sous Licence Microsoft au CANADA :

DÉNI DE GARANTIES. Dans la mesure maximale permise par les lois applicables, le Contenu Sous Licence et les services de soutien technique (le cas échéant) sont fournis *TELS QUELS ET AVEC TOUS LES DÉFAUTS* par Microsoft et ses fournisseurs, lesquels par les présentes dénient toutes autres garanties et conditions expresses, implicites ou en vertu de la loi, notamment, mais sans limitation, (le cas échéant) les garanties, devoirs ou conditions implicites de qualité marchande, d'adaptation à une fin usage particulière, de fiabilité ou de disponibilité, d'exactitude ou d'exhaustivité des réponses, des résultats, des efforts déployés selon les règles de l'art, d'absence de virus et d'absence de négligence, le tout à l'égard du Contenu Sous Licence et de la prestation des services de soutien technique ou de l'omission de la 'une telle prestation des services de soutien technique ou à l'égard de la fourniture ou de l'omission de la fourniture de tous autres services, renseignements, Contenus Sous Licence, et contenu qui s'y rapporte grâce au Contenu Sous Licence ou provenant autrement de l'utilisation du Contenu Sous Licence. PAR AILLEURS, IL N'Y A AUCUNE GARANTIE OU CONDITION QUANT AU TITRE DE PROPRIÉTÉ, À LA JOUISSANCE OU LA POSSESSION PAISIBLE, À LA CONCORDANCE À UNE DESCRIPTION NI QUANT À UNE ABSENCE DE CONTREFAÇON CONCERNANT LE CONTENU SOUS LICENCE.

EXCLUSION DES DOMMAGES ACCESSOIRES, INDIRECTS ET DE CERTAINS AUTRES DOMMAGES. DANS LA MESURE MAXIMALE PERMISE PAR LES LOIS APPLICABLES, EN AUCUN CAS MICROSOFT OU SES FOURNISSEURS NE SERONT RESPONSABLES DES DOMMAGES SPÉCIAUX, CONSÉCUTIFS, ACCESSOIRES OU INDIRECTS DE QUELQUE NATURE QUE CE SOIT (NOTAMMENT, LES DOMMAGES À L'ÉGARD DU MANQUE À GAGNER OU DE LA DIVULGATION DE RENSEIGNEMENTS CONFIDENTIELS OU AUTRES, DE LA PERTE D'EXPLOITATION, DE BLESSURES CORPORELLES, DE LA VIOLATION DE LA VIE PRIVÉE, DE L'OMISSION DE REMPLIR TOUT DEVOIR, Y COMPRIS D'AGIR DE BONNE FOI OU D'EXERCER UN SOIN RAISONNABLE, DE LA NÉGLIGENCE ET DE TOUTE AUTRE PERTE PÉCUNIAIRE OU AUTRE PERTE

DE QUELQUE NATURE QUE CE SOIT) SE RAPPORTANT DE QUELQUE MANIÈRE QUE CE SOIT À L'UTILISATION DU CONTENU SOUS LICENCE OU À L'INCAPACITÉ DE S'EN SERVIR, À LA PRESTATION OU À L'OMISSION DE LA 'UNE TELLE PRESTATION DE SERVICES DE SOUTIEN TECHNIQUE OU À LA FOURNITURE OU À L'OMISSION DE LA FOURNITURE DE TOUS AUTRES SERVICES, RENSEIGNEMENTS, CONTENUS SOUS LICENCE, ET CONTENU QUI S'Y RAPPORTE GRÂCE AU CONTENU SOUS LICENCE OU PROVENANT AUTREMENT DE L'UTILISATION DU CONTENU SOUS LICENCE OU AUTREMENT AUX TERMES DE TOUTE DISPOSITION DE LA U PRÉSENTE CONVENTION EULA OU RELATIVEMENT À UNE TELLE DISPOSITION, MÊME EN CAS DE FAUTE, DE DÉLIT CIVIL (Y COMPRIS LA NÉGLIGENCE), DE RESPONSABILITÉ STRICTE, DE VIOLATION DE CONTRAT OU DE VIOLATION DE GARANTIE DE MICROSOFT OU DE TOUT FOURNISSEUR ET MÊME SI MICROSOFT OU TOUT FOURNISSEUR A ÉTÉ AVISÉ DE LA POSSIBILITÉ DE TELS DOMMAGES.

<u>LIMITATION DE RESPONSABILITÉ ET RECOURS.</u>   MALGRÉ LES DOMMAGES QUE VOUS PUISSIEZ SUBIR POUR QUELQUE MOTIF QUE CE SOIT (NOTAMMENT, MAIS SANS LIMITATION, TOUS LES DOMMAGES SUSMENTIONNÉS ET TOUS LES DOMMAGES DIRECTS OU GÉNÉRAUX OU AUTRES), LA SEULE RESPONSABILITÉ 'OBLIGATION INTÉGRALE DE MICROSOFT ET DE L'UN OU L'AUTRE DE SES FOURNISSEURS AUX TERMES DE TOUTE DISPOSITION DEU LA PRÉSENTE CONVENTION EULA ET VOTRE RECOURS EXCLUSIF À L'ÉGARD DE TOUT CE QUI PRÉCÈDE SE LIMITE AU PLUS ÉLEVÉ ENTRE LES MONTANTS SUIVANTS : LE MONTANT QUE VOUS AVEZ RÉELLEMENT PAYÉ POUR LE CONTENU SOUS LICENCE OU 5,00 $US. LES LIMITES, EXCLUSIONS ET DÉNIS QUI PRÉCÈDENT (Y COMPRIS LES CLAUSES CI-DESSUS), S'APPLIQUENT DANS LA MESURE MAXIMALE PERMISE PAR LES LOIS APPLICABLES, MÊME SI TOUT RECOURS N'ATTEINT PAS SON BUT ESSENTIEL.

À moins que cela ne soit prohibé par le droit local applicable, la présente Convention est régie par les lois de la province d'Ontario, Canada. Vous consentez Chacune des parties à la présente reconnaît irrévocablement à la compétence des tribunaux fédéraux et provinciaux siégeant à Toronto, dans de la province d'Ontario et consent à instituer tout litige qui pourrait découler de la présente auprès des tribunaux situés dans le district judiciaire de York, province d'Ontario.

Au cas où vous auriez des questions concernant cette licence ou que vous désiriez vous mettre en rapport avec Microsoft pour quelque raison que ce soit, veuillez utiliser l'information contenue dans le Contenu Sous Licence pour contacter la filiale de succursale Microsoft desservant votre pays, dont l'adresse est fournie dans ce produit, ou visitez écrivez à : Microsoft sur le World Wide Web à http://www.microsoft.com

Contents

Unit 1: Introduction to Troubleshooting Exchange Server 2003

Using Service Logs

By default, services that log activity store their logs in the *systemroot*\system32\logfiles folder.

The Web, SMTP, and NNTP logs are especially relevant to Exchange troubleshooting. For example, if your server is unable to transmit messages to a remote server across the Internet, you may wish to enable SMTP logging so that you can review the SMTP activity between the two servers.

The DNS log is located in the *systemroot*\system32\dns folder. The DNS log file maintains DNS error messages.

Moving Logs

Most of the log files can be moved by making changes in the properties of the service. For example, in **Exchange System Manager**, you can expand the **Server** and the **Protocols** nodes, and then expand the **SMTP** node. Right-click **Default SMTP Virtual Server** and click **Properties**.

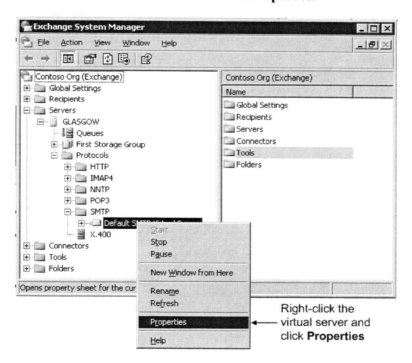

Right-click the virtual server and click **Properties**

Select the check box to **Enable logging**, and click **Properties** to make changes as needed.

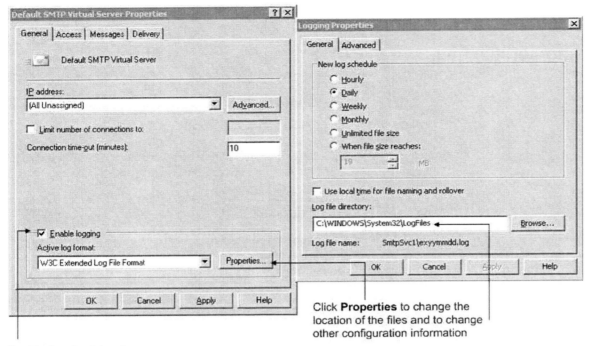

Enable the check box to
enable logging for the service

Click **Properties** to change the
location of the files and to change
other configuration information

Unit 2: Troubleshooting Network Connectivity

Internet E-Mail Testing Methods

One of the easier troubleshooting tasks for a Microsoft® Exchange Server 2003 server administrator is to troubleshoot Internet e-mail problems. There are two main methods of basic troubleshooting: using an Internet Web-based e-mail application and using Telnet.

Using Hotmail

You will need a Web-based e-mail account, such as a Microsoft Hotmail® account (http://www.hotmail.com), that you can use for troubleshooting purposes.

Testing the Ability to Send E-Mail from the Company to the Internet

The best way to test the ability of your company to send e-mail to the Internet is to send a message to the Internet and see if it arrives. Send an e-mail from your company account to your Web-based e-mail account. If your Web-based e-mail account receives the e-mail, you know that your company can send e-mail to Internet recipients. Your Exchange Server 2003 server does not have a problem sending e-mail to the Internet.

Testing the Ability to Receive E-Mail from the Internet to the Company

You can use a similar approach to test whether your company is able to receive Internet e-mail. Send a message from your Web-based e-mail account to your company account and see if it arrives in a timely fashion. (You might want to have several different Web-based e-mail accounts since delivery through these systems sometimes can be slow.) If the e-mail arrives, you know that your company can receive Internet e-mail. If the e-mail does not arrive, you will have to then troubleshoot the reason that e-mail is not being received from the Internet. The most common reasons for this are that the mail exchanger (MX) record and the A record are not correct or that the firewall is blocking port 25 inbound.

Using Telnet

Using Telnet is a little more difficult because it is not graphical.

Testing the Ability to Send E-Mail from the Company to the Internet

Using Telnet, you can test connectivity from your Exchange Server 2003 server to another e-mail server on the Internet. If you know of another company that has an Internet e-mail server, open a command prompt on the Exchange Server 2003 server and type **Telnet** *companyx.com* **25** (where *companyx.com* is the domain name of the target company that accepts Internet e-mail). If the remote system replies, your company's ability to send e-mail to the Internet is confirmed. Check with several Internet e-mail servers to make sure your messaging environment is properly configured.

Testing the Ability to Receive E-Mail from the Internet to the Company

Using Telnet, you can test connectivity from another computer (it doesn't have to be an e-mail server) to your Exchange server. The problem with this process is that very few people have access to an account on a remote computer. If you have the ability to connect remotely to another computer, you can test the ability of your server to receive e-mail from the Internet. Open a command prompt on the remote computer and type **Telnet** *companyz.com* **25** (where *companyz.com* is your company domain name). If your server replies, your company's ability to receive e-mail from the Internet is confirmed.

Impact of Virus and Content Scanners on Messaging Functionality

One of the more difficult components to troubleshoot in messaging is third-party scanning software. Messages need to be scanned in order to stop virus infections and the propagation of virus infections to other e-mail systems on the Internet.

Over the past couple of years, companies have started to realize that their e-mail servers are being clogged with non-business related e-mail (e.g., personal e-mail between friends), Unsolicited Commercial E-mail (UCE; also known as spam), and even e-mail that is meant to maliciously harm the company.

Virus infections

Virus infections are bad news for a number of reasons:

- Lost productivity of end-users
- Poor server performance (the Melissa virus is a great example)
- Inability to process important business messages
- Spreading the virus to other companies can cause a temporary e-mail block
- Publicity that impacts the stock value of a company

To prevent virus infections, antivirus software must be kept up to date. Antivirus software usually exists in several places in a company, including:

- *Firewalls or viruswalls.* Firewalls and viruswalls can be troublesome, as many of them do not support all of the Simple Mail Transfer Protocol (SMTP) verbs available and may cause problems depending on the origination system and the type of message being sent.
- *E-mail servers.* Most antivirus software packages will scan the stores on a regular basis and will scan all new messages as they arrive.
- *File servers.* Users often pull attachments from file servers, and it is important to know that they will be virus free before they are sent.
- *Client computers.* In the event a virus gets past any of the other antivirus applications, you need to be aware that a client-side antivirus application may end up deleting messages through the Outlook client.

Content scanning

Content scanning is not just looking for virus-infected files. Content scanning is utilized by many companies to:

- Combat SPAM.
- Keep users from sending proprietary information outside the company.
- Keep users from sending explicit e-mails to others.
- Keep outside e-mail that may lead to sexual harassment concerns from being sent to users.

The problem that occurs most often with content scanning is that many false positives can occur, leading to lost productivity and a great deal of administrative effort to fix the scanning solution.

Performance impact

While it is acknowledged that virus and content scanners are needed in many cases, the related performance decreases can be very significant. You might need to install extra CPUs and RAM to handle the load placed by these scanners on your e-mail server.

Administrative impact

You also need to be aware that positive scanner hits, as well as false positive hits, will mean that some messages are being lost. Some users will assume something is wrong with the e-mail server when they do not get the e-mails they are expecting, and this can lead to extra, unnecessary troubleshooting work since there is not a problem with your e-mail server. Be ready to check quarantine logs for messages as part of the troubleshooting process for lost messages.

Using the Telnet Command to Test the TCP Port Restrictions on a Firewall

If you feel that the firewall might be the source of a problem, you can use Telnet to test the firewall port restrictions. From inside the firewall to the Internet, you will need to find a server that will accept your session. For example, if you want to test whether SMTP is open and allowing traffic from inside the network to outside the network, you will need to have a target system somewhere outside the firewall that will accept SMTP commands. Basically, this is any e-mail server on the Internet. To test SMTP, use the following steps:

Test SMTP – Port 25

1. Click **Start**, click **Run**, type **CMD** and then click **OK**.

2. At the command prompt, type **telnet** *company.com* **25** (where *company.com* is the domain name of the e-mail server) and wait for the response.

   If the target is an Exchange Server 2003 server with a properly configured MX record and the firewall allows port 25 traffic outside the company, you will receive the following message:

   220 *company.com* (where *company.com* is the domain name of the e-mail server) Microsoft ESMTP MAIL Service, Version: 6.0.3790.0 ready at Sun, 10 Aug 2003 04:08:26 -0600

3. Type **quit** at the prompt to close the connection.

You can use this same procedure from outside the company to test your firewall and make sure that port 25 is open to allow incoming e-mail traffic.

Test POP3 – Port 110 and 995

Generally, you will only allow remote network users to access Exchange Server 2003 using Post Office Protocol version 3 (POP3),since internal clients will be better served using the Outlook client. To test POP3 from outside the firewall, use the following steps:

1. Click **Start**, click **Run**, type **CMD** and then click **OK**.

2. At the command prompt, type **telnet** *company.com* **110** (where *company.com* is the domain name of the e-mail server) and wait for the response.

   If the target is an Exchange Server 2003 server and the firewall allows port 110 traffic from outside the company, you will receive the following message:

   +OK Microsoft Exchange Server 2003 POP3 server version 6.5.6944.0 *company.com* (where *company.com* is the domain name of the e-mail server) ready.

3. Type **quit** at the prompt to close the connection.

4. Test 995, which is used for Secure Sockets Layer (SSL) protected POP3 services, using the same process, but typing **995** instead of 110.

Test IMAP4 – Port 143 and 993

Generally, you will only allow remote network users to access Exchange Server 2003 using Internet Message Access Protocol version 4rev1 (IMAP4), since internal clients will be better served using the Outlook client. To test IMAP4 from outside the firewall, use the following steps:

1. Click **Start**, click **Run**, type **CMD** and then click **OK**.

2. At the command prompt, type **telnet** *company.com* **143** (where *company.com* is the domain name of the e-mail server) and wait for the response.

   If the target is an Exchange 2003 server and the firewall allows port 143 traffic from outside the company, you will receive the following message:

   * OK Microsoft Exchange Server 2003 IMAP4rev1 server version 6.5.6944.0 *company.com* (where *company.com* is the domain name of the e-mail server) ready.

3. Type **IMAP Logout** at the prompt to close the connection.

4. Test 993, which is used for SSL-protected IMAP4 services, using the same process, typing **993** instead of 143.

Other ports

You can use Telnet to test the firewall to see if other ports are open and verify that the server responds to the traffic type used by the port. For example, you can test Network News Transfer Protocol (NNTP) port availability to use port number 119. Once connected, you can send NNTP commands and verify that NNTP is functioning as expected.

Updating the Global Address List (GAL)

What is the GAL?

The global address list (GAL) contains all the addresses that have been created and entered in the Exchange Server 2003 server when mailboxes were created for users, e-mail addresses were created for public folders, and directory information was imported from external messaging systems.

The Recipient Update Service interacts with Microsoft Active Directory® to populate the **showInAddressBook** attribute for all objects that have a **mailNickname** attribute. The Recipient Update Service will not populate the **showInAddressBook** attribute if the **msExchHideFromAddressLists** attribute is set to TRUE.

When Outlook tries to resolve a name, it will search the GAL for a name that matches the query. If the query is looking for a name that is not populated with an address list in the **showInAddressBook**, resolution will fail and the mailbox will not be able to be contacted unless you know its name.

Updating the GAL

Updating the GAL can be done by forcing the Recipient Update Service to update or rebuild, using the following steps:

1. Click **Start**, click **All Programs**, click **Microsoft Exchange**, and then click **System Manager**.
2. Expand the Recipients node by double-clicking it.
3. Expand the Recipient Policies node by double-clicking it.
4. Right-click the **Default Policy** and select **Apply this policy now**.
5. Expand the Recipients Update Service node by double-clicking it.
6. Right-click the Recipient Update Service for the domain that you want to update.
7. Click **Update Now**.
8. The update will begin immediately. Close all open windows.

Note: If you click **Rebuild** instead of **Update Now**, it will take longer to fully update the GAL. However, it might be a good idea to perform a rebuild if you have made a large number of updates.

Using Dcdiag and Netdiag to Verify the Network Infrastructure

The DCDiag command

DCDiag will perform the following:

- Verify that the domain can support Active Directory.
- Determine if it is possible to create an Active Directory forest.
- Determine if it is possible to add another domain controller to an existing domain.
- Determine if a Microsoft Windows 2000, Microsoft Windows XP, or Microsoft Windows Server™ 2003 computer can be added to the domain.
- Test replication between domain controllers.
- Report down servers.
- Test that all domain controllers are advertising their presence to other domain controllers.

DCDiag can be used to test the state of domain controllers in a forest. It will report any problems it finds.

/v   Verbose mode will provide more information in an easier-to-read format. The /v switch will also provide information about the Flexible Single Master Operation (FSMO) roles.

/f   The /f switch is used to point to a file for logging the results of the DCDiag command.

/?   The help switch will provide more information about the other options that are available for the DCDiag command.

The NetDiag command

NetDiag tests network connectivity by testing the following items:

- Network adapter interface information, including the:
  - Host name
  - IP address
  - Subnet mask
  - Default gateway
  - DNS server
  - Windows Internet Name Service (WINS) server
- Domain membership
- Loopback ping test
- Default gateway ping test
- Network basic input/output system (NetBIOS) name check
- Winsock test
- DNS test

- Domain controller discovery test
- Trust relationship test
- Lightweight Directory Access Protocol (LDAP) test
- Internet Protocol Security (IPSec) test

/v   The tests performed by NetDiag will alert you to many possible problems. You can expand on the result messages by using the /v switch to turn on verbose mode.

/f   The tests performed by NetDiag can result in a large amount of output. It may be necessary to send the resulting information to others to review. Using the /l switch will capture the information to a log file in the same directory as the netdiag.exe file.

/?   The help switch will provide more information about the other options that are available for the NetDiag command.

Verifying That a Server is Online

During troubleshooting, you may need to verify remotely that a server is online. This verification can include several steps. In most cases, you should start by verifying basic network connectivity and then verify name resolution, and then verify service availability.

1. To verify network connectivity, ping the IP address of the remote server. If the ping is successful, move on to the next step in troubleshooting. If the ping is not successful, determine whether there is a network failure by pinging another server in the same subnet, or by using pathping or tracert to determine where the failure occurs.

2. If the ping is successful, ping the fully qualified domain name of the server. If the ping is successful, move on to the next step. If the ping is not successful, then use tools such as NSLookup or DNSLint to determine the DNS zone information and server configuration. You may also need to check the Hosts file—in most cases; the hosts file should not contain any information.

3. In some cases, clients may need to connect to the server using NetBIOS names. This is true if you have older clients such as Windows 95, Windows 98 or Windows NT workstations on your network. To verify NetBIOS connectivity, use the Net Use command, or use Netdiag.exe. You can also use the Browstat.exe command (included in the Windows Server 2003 Support Tools) to perform detailed troubleshooting of NetBIOS browser troubleshooting.

4. If you can successfully connect to the server using host and NetBIOS names, then the next step in troubleshooting is to test protocol connectivity. The best tool to test email related protocol connectivity is Telnet. If you cannot connect to the server using Telnet, verify that the required protocol is not blocked by a network device.

5. If you cannot connect to the server using Telnet, confirm that the required services are running on the Exchange server. The services that must be running on a front-end server are discussed in the Securing a Front-End and Back-End Server Infrastructure toolkit resource. The following services must be running on a back-end server:

   - Microsoft Exchange System Attendant
   - Microsoft Exchange Information Store
   - Microsoft Exchange Management
   - Windows Management Instrumentation
   - Microsoft Exchange Routing Engine
   - IIS Admin Service
   - SMTP
   - World Wide Web Publishing Service
   - Additional services, like NNTP, Microsoft Exchange IMAP4, Microsoft Exchange POP3, HTTP SSL Microsoft Exchange Event Service, Microsoft Exchange Site Replication Service, Exchange MTA Stacks may be required to support Internet protocol clients or for compatibility with previous versions of Exchange.

Note   These services are dependant on Windows Server 2003 services. View the properties of each service to confirm the service dependencies.

To verify the status of the services on a remote computer, you can connect to the computer using a custom Computer Management MMC or use Remote Desktop. If the required services are functional on the server, verify that the Exchange mailbox and public folder stores are mounted. You can use the Exchange System Manager to verify the mounted stores.

Unit 3: Troubleshooting Public Folders and Mailboxes

Impact of Virus and Content Scanners on Messaging Functionality

One of the more difficult components to troubleshoot in messaging is third-party scanning software. Messages need to be scanned in order to stop virus infections and the propagation of virus infections to other e-mail systems on the Internet.

Over the past couple of years, companies have started to realize that their e-mail servers are being clogged with non-business related e-mail (e.g., personal e-mail between friends), Unsolicited Commercial E-mail (UCE; also known as spam), and even e-mail that is meant to maliciously harm the company.

Virus infections

Virus infections are bad news for a number of reasons:

- Lost productivity of end-users
- Poor server performance (the Melissa virus is a great example)
- Unable to process our important business messages
- Spreading the virus to other companies can cause a temporary e-mail block
- Publicity that impacts the stock value of a company

To prevent virus infections, antivirus software must be kept up to date. Antivirus software usually exists in several places in a company, including:

- *Firewalls or viruswalls*. Firewalls and viruswalls can be troublesome, as many of them do not support all of the Simple Mail Transfer Protocol (SMTP) verbs available and may cause problems depending on the origination system and the type of message being sent.
- *E-mail servers*. Most antivirus software packages will scan the stores on a regular basis and will scan all new messages as they arrive.
- *File servers*. Users often pull attachments from file servers, so it is important to know that they will be virus free before they are sent.
- *Client computers*. In the event a virus gets past any of the other antivirus applications, you need to be aware that a client-side antivirus application may end up deleting messages through the Outlook client.

Content scanning

Content scanning is not just looking for virus infected files. Content scanning is utilized by many companies to:

- Combat SPAM.
- Keep users from sending proprietary information outside the company.
- Keep users from sending explicit e-mails to others.
- Keep outside e-mail that may lead to sexual harassment concerns from being sent to users.

The problem that occurs most often with content scanning is that many false positives can occur, leading to lost productivity and a great deal of administrative effort to fix the scanning solution.

Performance impact   While it is acknowledged that virus and content scanners are needed in many cases, the related performance decreases can be very significant. You might need to install extra CPUs and RAM to handle the load placed on your e-mail server by these scanners.

Administrative impact   You also need to be aware that positive scanner hits, as well as false positive hits, will mean that some messages are being lost. Some users will assume something is wrong with the e-mail server when they do not get the e-mails they are expecting, and this can lead to extra, unnecessary troubleshooting work since there is not a problem with your e-mail server. Be ready to check quarantine logs for messages as part of the troubleshooting process for lost messages.

Using the Telnet Command to Test Connectivity Between Exchange Servers

The Telnet command is very useful for troubleshooting protocol level connectivity. Using Telnet, you can specify which port you wish to use to connect to another server. For example, you can test for SMTP connectivity by attempting a connection to TCP/IP port 25. If the connection is successful, you will have confirmed that you have TCP/IP connectivity as well as SMTP connectivity. If you use the fully qualified domain name of the destination Microsoft® Exchange Server 2003 server, you will also have confirmed DNS name resolution.

To use Telnet to test SMTP connectivity between Vancouver.NWTraders1.msft and Denver.NWTraders1.msft, follow these steps:

1. Log on to one of the Exchange servers. You can log on locally or use the Remote Desktop.

2. Click **Start**, click **Run**, type **CMD** and click **OK**.

3. At the command prompt, type **telnet Denver.NWTraders1.msft 25** and wait for the response.

4. If you can connect to the Exchange server using port 25, you will receive the following message:

   220 Denver.NWTraders1.msft Microsoft ESMTP MAIL Service, Version: 6.0.3790.0 ready at Wed, 13 Aug 2003 14:08:26 -0600

5. Type **quit** at the prompt to close the connection.

If you cannot connect using this procedure, try connecting to the IP address of the destination server. If this is successful, check the DNS configuration. If you cannot connect using the IP address, try to ping the destination server. If you can ping the server but cannot connect using SMTP, troubleshoot the SMTP service on the destination server.

Using the Telnet Command to Test the TCP Port Restrictions on a Firewall

If you feel that the firewall might be the source of a problem, you can use Telnet to test the firewall port restrictions. From inside the firewall to the Internet, you will need to find a server that will accept your session. For example, if you want to test whether SMTP is open and allowing traffic from inside the network to outside the network, you will need to have a target system somewhere outside the firewall that will accept SMTP commands. Basically, this is any e-mail server on the Internet. To test SMTP, use the following steps:

Test SMTP – Port 25

1. Click **Start**, click **Run**, type **CMD** and then click **OK**.

2. At the command prompt, type **telnet** *company.com* **25** (where *company.com* is the domain name of the e-mail server) and wait for the response.

   If the target is an Exchange Server 2003 server with a properly configured MX record and the firewall allows port 25 traffic outside the company, you will receive the following message:

   220 *company.com* (where *company.com* is the domain name of the e-mail server) Microsoft ESMTP MAIL Service, Version: 6.0.3790.0 ready at Sun, 10 Aug 2003 04:08:26 -0600

3. Type **quit** at the prompt to close the connection.

You can use this same procedure from outside the company to test the firewall and make sure port 25 is open to allow incoming e-mail traffic.

Test POP3 – Port 110 and 995

Generally, you will only allow remote network users to access Exchange Server 2003 using Post Office Protocol version 3 (POP3), since internal clients will be better served using the Outlook client. To test POP3 from outside the firewall, use the following steps:

1. Click **Start**, click **Run**, type **CMD** and then click **OK**.

2. At the command prompt, type **telnet** *company.com* **110** (where *company.com* is the domain name of the e-mail server) and wait for the response.

   If the target is an Exchange Server 2003 server and the firewall allows port 110 traffic from outside the company, you will receive the following message:

   +OK Microsoft Exchange Server 2003 POP3 server version 6.5.6944.0 *company.com* (where *company.com* is the domain name of the e-mail server) ready

3. Type **quit** at the prompt to close the connection.

4. Test 995, which is used for Secure Sockets Layer- (SSL) protected POP3 services, using the same process, but typing **995** instead of 110.

Test IMAP4 – Port 143 and 993

Generally, you will only allow remote network users to access Exchange Server 2003 using Internet Message Access Protocol version 4rev1 (IMAP4), since internal clients will be better served using the Outlook client. To test from outside of the firewall, use the following steps:

1. Click **Start**, click **Run**, type **CMD** and then click **OK**.

2. At the command prompt, type **telnet** *company.com* **143** (where *company.com* is the domain name of the e-mail server) and wait for the response.

   If the target is an Exchange 2003 server and the firewall allows port 143 traffic from outside the company, you will receive the following message:

   * OK Microsoft Exchange Server 2003 IMAP4rev1 server version 6.5.6944.0 *company.com* (where *company.com* is the domain name of the e-mail server) ready

3. Type **IMAP Logout** at the prompt to close the connection.

4. Test 993, which is used for SSL-protected IMAP4 services, using the same process, typing **993** instead of 143.

Other ports

You can use Telnet to test the firewall to see if other ports are open and verify that the server responds to the traffic type used by the port. For example, you can test Network News Transfer Protocol (NNTP) port availability to use port number 119. Once connected, you can send NNTP commands and verify that NNTP is functioning as expected.

Updating the Global Address List

What is the GAL?

The global address list (GAL) contains all the addresses that have been created and entered in the Exchange Server 2003 server when mailboxes were created for users, e-mail addresses were created for public folders, and directory information was imported from external messaging systems.

The Recipient Update Service interacts with Microsoft Active Directory® to populate the **showInAddressBook** attribute for all objects that have a **mailNickname** attribute. The Recipient Update Service will not populate the **showInAddressBook** attribute if the **msExchHideFromAddressLists** attribute is set to TRUE.

When Microsoft Outlook® tries to resolve a name, it will search the GAL for a name that matches the query. If the query is looking for a name that is not populated with an address list in the **showInAddressBook**, resolution will fail and the mailbox will not be able to be contacted unless you know its name.

Updating the GAL

Updating the GAL can be done by forcing the Recipient Update Service to update or rebuild, using the following steps:

1. Click **Start**, click **All Programs**, click **Microsoft Exchange**, and then click **System Manager**.
2. Expand the Recipients node by double-clicking it.
3. Expand the Recipient Policies node by double-clicking it.
4. Right-click the **Default Policy** and select **Apply this policy now**.
5. Expand the Recipients Update Service node by double-clicking it.
6. Right-click the **Recipient Update Service** for the domain that you want to update.
7. Click **Update Now**.
8. The update will begin immediately. Close all open windows.

Note: If you click **Rebuild** instead of **Update Now**, it will take longer to fully update the GAL. However, it might be a good idea to perform a rebuild if you have made a large number of updates.

Configuring the Recipient Update Service

The Recipient Update Service updates the address lists in Exchange Server 2003 as well as the e-mail addresses for Exchange recipients. You can modify the Recipient Update Service by specifying which domain controller and which Exchange server will be used by the service and how often the service will run.

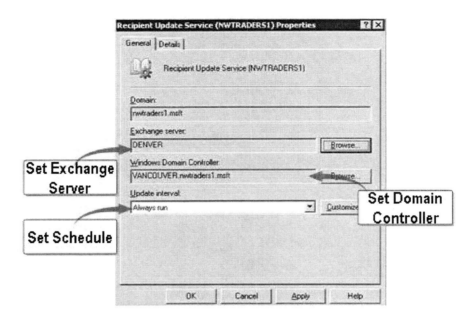

Use the following procedure to configure the Recipient Update Service:

1. In the Exchange System Manager console tree, browse to Recipients\Recipient Update Services and click **Recipient Update Service**.

2. In the details pane, right-click **Recipient Update Service (NWTRADERS)** and then click **Properties**.

3. Click **Browse** to change the Exchange server or Windows domain controller settings. Type the name of the server you want to use, and then click **OK**.

4. Chose an Update interval. You can configure the Recipient Update Service to always run; to run at 1-, 2-, or 4-hour intervals; or to never run. You can also configure a custom schedule.

5. When you have completed the configuration, click **OK**.

Viewing Recipient Policies

Exchange Server 2003 uses recipient policies to set e-mail addresses and to configure mailbox manager policies. When you configure a recipient policy, you must configure a Lightweight Directory Access Protocol (LDAP) query that identifies the recipients that will be affected by the policy and specifies the e-mail addresses that will be applied to the recipients. You can also configure a priority level for the recipient policies.

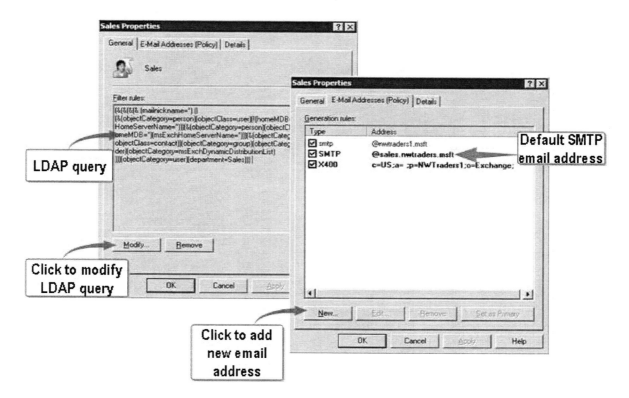

To view recipient policy properties, use the following procedure:

1. In the Exchange System Manager console tree, browse to Recipients and expand the Recipient Policies container.

2. Select a recipient policy, and then click **Properties**.

   The **General** tab displays the LDAP query that is associated with this policy. You can modify the LDAP query by clicking **Modify**.

   The **E-Mail Addresses (Policy)** tab displays the e-mail addresses that are associated with this policy. You can add additional e-mail addresses, edit or remove existing e-mail addresses, or set an e-mail address as the primary e-mail address by clicking **New**.

3. Click **OK**.

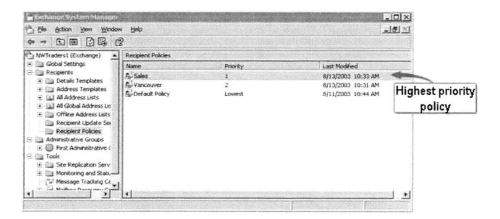

4. The order in which recipient policies are applied is set by configuring a priority level to each policy. The policies are applied from the bottom of the list upwards. To modify the order, right-click a recipient policy, click **All Tasks**, and then click **Move Up** or **Move Down**.

Viewing Delivery Restrictions on SMTP Connectors

One reason why a user cannot send and receive Internet e-mail may be the delivery restrictions on the SMTP connector that is used to send and receive e-mail from the Internet. These delivery restrictions can be used to limit which users can send e-mail using the SMTP connector, and therefore can restrict users from sending e-mail to the Internet. The SMTP connector can also be configured to limit the size of messages that can be sent using the connector. This size limitation applies to messages sent in both directions on the SMTP connector.

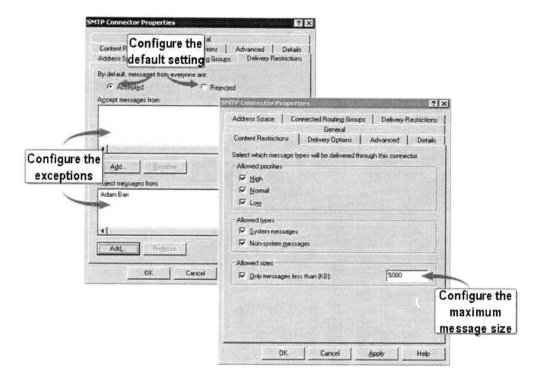

To view the properties of an SMTP connector, follow this procedure:

1. In Exchange System Manager, expand the Administrative Groups container and then expand the specific administrative group.

2. Expand the Routing Groups container, and then expand the specific routing group.

3. Expand the Connectors container. Right-click the **SMTP connector** and click **Properties**.

4. The **Delivery Restrictions** tab is used to limit who can send e-mail using this connector. You must first identify the default setting for the connector by determining if messages sent by everyone are accepted (allowed) or rejected (not allowed). Then you can configure the exceptions to the default rule. For example, if you allow everyone to use the connector, you need to configure those accounts that should not be allowed to send mail using the connector.

5. The **Content Restrictions** tab is used to configure the maximum message size that can be sent using the connector. To enable this, you must select **Only messages less than (KB)** and then specify a maximum message size.

Internet E-Mail Testing Methods

One of the easier troubleshooting tasks for a Microsoft® Exchange Server 2003 server administrator is to troubleshoot Internet e-mail problems. There are two main methods of basic troubleshooting: using an Internet Web-based e-mail application and using Telnet.

Using Hotmail

You will need a Web-based e-mail account, such as a Microsoft Hotmail® account (http://www.hotmail.com), that you can use for troubleshooting purposes.

Testing the Ability to Send E-Mail from the Company to the Internet

The best way to test the ability of your company to send e-mail to the Internet is to send a message to the Internet and see if it arrives. Send an e-mail from your company account to your Web-based e-mail account. If your Web-based e-mail account receives the e-mail, you know that your company can send e-mail to Internet recipients. Your Exchange Server 2003 server does not have a problem sending e-mail to the Internet.

Testing the Ability to Receive E-Mail from the Internet to the Company

You can use a similar approach to test whether your company is able to receive Internet e-mail. Send a message from your Web-based e-mail account to your company account and see if it arrives in a timely fashion. (You might want to have several different Web-based e-mail accounts since delivery through these systems sometimes can be slow.) If the e-mail arrives, you know that your company can receive Internet e-mail. If the e-mail does not arrive, you will have to then troubleshoot the reason that e-mail is not being received from the Internet. The most common reasons for this are that the mail exchanger (MX) record and the A record are not correct or that the firewall is blocking port 25 inbound.

Using Telnet

Using Telnet is a little more difficult because it is not graphical.

Testing the Ability to Send E-Mail from the Company to the Internet

Using Telnet, you can test connectivity from your Exchange Server 2003 server to another e-mail server on the Internet. If you know of another company that has an Internet e-mail server, open a command prompt on the Exchange Server 2003 server and type **Telnet** *companyx.com* **25** (where *companyx.com* is the domain name of the target company that accepts Internet e-mail). If the remote system replies, your company's ability to send e-mail to the Internet is confirmed. Check with several Internet e-mail servers to make sure your messaging environment is properly configured.

Testing the Ability to Receive E-Mail from the Internet to the Company

Using Telnet, you can test connectivity from another computer (it doesn't have to be an e-mail server) to your Exchange server. The problem with this process is that very few people have access to an account on a remote computer. If you have the ability to connect remotely to another computer, you can test the ability of your server to receive e-mail from the Internet. Open a command prompt on the remote computer and type **Telnet** *companyz.com* **25** (where *companyz.com* is your company domain name). If your server replies, your company's ability to receive e-mail from the Internet is confirmed.

Using Dcdiag and Netdiag to Verify the Network Infrastructure

The DCDiag command   DCDiag will perform the following:

- Verify that the domain can support Active Directory.

- Determine if it is possible to create an Active Directory forest.

- Determine if it is possible to add another domain controller to an existing domain.

- Determine if a Microsoft Windows 2000, Microsoft Windows XP, or Microsoft Windows Server™ 2003 computer can be added to the domain.

- Test replication between domain controllers.

- Report down servers.

- Test that all domain controllers are advertising their presence to other domain controllers.

DCDiag can be used to test the state of domain controllers in a forest. It will report any problems it finds.

/v   Verbose mode will provide more information in an easier-to-read format. The /v switch will also provide information about the Flexible Single Master Operation (FSMO) roles.

/f   The /f switch is used to point to a file for logging the results of the DCDiag command.

/?   The help switch will provide more information about the other options that are available for the DCDiag command.

The NetDiag command   NetDiag tests network connectivity by testing the following items:

- Network adapter interface information, including the:
  - Host name
  - IP address
  - Subnet mask
  - Default gateway
  - DNS server
  - Windows Internet Name Service (WINS) server
- Domain membership
- Loopback ping test
- Default gateway ping test
- Network basic input/output system (NetBIOS) name check
- Winsock test
- DNS test

- Domain controller discovery test
- Trust relationship test
- Lightweight Directory Access Protocol (LDAP) test
- Internet Protocol Security (IPSec) test

/v   The tests performed by NetDiag will alert you to many possible problems. You can expand on the result messages by using the /v switch to turn on verbose mode.

/f   The tests performed by NetDiag can result in a large amount of output. It may be necessary to send the resulting information to others to review. Using the /l switch will capture the information to a log file in the same directory as the netdiag.exe file.

/?   The help switch will provide more information about the other options that are available for the NetDiag command.

Unit 4: Troubleshooting Outlook Web Access and Outlook Mobile Access

Firewall Configuration Required to Support Front-End and Back-End Servers

In order to deploy Microsoft® Outlook® Web Access (OWA) and Microsoft Outlook Mobile Access (OMA) securely, you must use one or more firewalls to protect the Microsoft Exchange Server 2003 servers from Internet traffic. In most cases, the recommended firewall configuration is a perimeter network.

In this configuration, there is a firewall connected directly to the Internet. Behind this firewall, there is a screened subnet that is isolated from the internal company network by a second internal firewall. The front-end servers are located in the perimeter network, and the back-end servers are located on the internal network. With this firewall configuration, you can open one very limited set of ports on the Internet firewall and a different set of ports on the internal firewall.

Internet firewall configuration

If you use a perimeter network, you will need to open ports on the firewall that is located between the Internet and the perimeter network. These ports must be open so that the OWA client can connect to the front-end server from the Internet. If you are using the front-end server only for OWA and OMA, you should open only port 80 for HTTP and only port 443 for HTTP with Secure Sockets Layer (SSL). Any additional ports should be enabled only if the server is also operating as the front-end server for additional protocols.

Internal firewall ports

When you use a perimeter network, you also need to open ports on the firewall between the front-end server and the back-end servers and domain controllers. Open ports between the front-end server and servers on the intranet as described in the following table.

Service	Port number	Requirement
HTTP	TCP port 80	Used by the front-end server to communicate with the back-end server. SSL is not supported.
LDAP to domain controller	TCP port 389 and UDP port 389	Used by the front-end server to query a domain controller on the internal network.
LDAP to global catalog server	TCP port 3268	Used by the front-end server to query a global catalog server on the internal network.
Kerberos	TCP port 88 and UDP port 88	Used by the front-end server to authenticate connections to the back-end servers and to the domain controllers.
DNS Lookup	TCP port 53 and UDP port 53	Used by the front-end server to locate computers on the internal network.
RPC port endpoint mapper	TCP port 135	Used by the front-end server to create a remote procedure call (RPC) session with a server on the internal network. RPCs are used for client authentication and to discover services on the internal network.
RPC service ports	TCP port 1024-65535 (this port can be statically assigned on global catalog servers through a registry key)	Used for RPC sessions between the front-end servers and back-end servers. The ports are dynamically assigned after the initial RPC connection on TCP port 135.

You can avoid having to open the DNS ports between the screened subnet and the internal network by configuring a DNS server on the front-end server or within the perimeter network. If you do configure a DNS server in the screened subnet, ensure that the zone files contain only the required records and that the DNS server cannot be accessed from the Internet. You cannot use host files, since you must have the appropriate service information for servers such as global catalog and Lightweight Directory Access Protocol (LDAP).

You can avoid having to open the RPC ports between the screened subnet and the internal network by configuring the front-end DNS server with the names of the domain controllers on the internal network. You can configure one or more domain controllers and global catalog servers on the **Directory Access** tab on the front-end server properties in Exchange System Manager.

Outlook Mobile Access Requirements

The architecture used to implement OMA is very similar to the architecture used to implement OWA. In both cases, clients use an HTML or HTML-based protocol to access a virtual directory on the default Web site on an Exchange server. Both OMA and OWA support the front-end back-end server topology. However, OMA does introduce some specific requirements in addition to the OWA requirements.

Server setup requirements

OMA is designed to take advantage of the Microsoft .NET Framework and Microsoft ASP.NET. The devices that are supported by Exchange Server 2003 for OMA are determined by the device update package that is installed on the Exchange 2003 server.

The three software components that are required for OMA in Exchange Server 2003 are:

- .NET Framework 1.1
- ASP.NET
- ASP.NET Device Update 2

The .NET Framework 1.1 is automatically installed on Microsoft Windows Server™ 2003. For Windows 2000 servers, SP3 or later, Exchange Setup automatically installs and enables both the .NET Framework and ASP.NET. Exchange Setup also installs the ASP.NET Device Update 2 package.

User configuration

In order for users to be able to access OMA, their user accounts must first be enabled for OMA. To configure user access to OMA, access the user account in Microsoft Active Directory® and use the **Exchange Features** tab to enable or disable the functionality for each user.

Securing Outlook Mobile Access

Like OWA, OMA passes all content to and from the Exchange servers in clear text, unless SSL enabled. To configure OMA to use SSL, you must install an SSL certificate on the server and configure an SSL certificate on the Outlook Mobile Access virtual directories in Internet Information Systems (IIS).

Securing a Front-End and Back-End Server Infrastructure

The OWA and OMA front-end servers must be deployed so that they are accessible from the Internet; therefore, it is essential that the servers be deployed as securely as possible. To ensure the security of OWA and OMA infrastructure, you must ensure that the servers and all network traffic are secure. The first step in securing the infrastructure is to enable only the required ports on both the Internet and internal firewalls. There are several additional steps that you can take to ensure maximum security.

Secure Internet network traffic

By default, all traffic between the Internet and the front-end server is sent in clear text, including user authentication traffic and messaging traffic. The easiest way to ensure that traffic is encrypted is to configure the front-end server to require SSL for all connections from the Internet. In most cases, you should configure the front-end server with a certificate from a commercial certificate authority to guarantee that the certificate is trusted on all Internet clients. If you require additional security and want to limit the client workstations that can be used, you can configure the front-end server to require client authentication and then provide certificates for all client workstations.

Disable services

To ensure that the front-end server is as secure as possible, disable all of the services that are not required on the server. The following table shows the services that must be running on the front-end server and the services that can be disabled.

Service name	Startup mode	Reason
Microsoft Exchange Routing Engine	Automatic	This service is required to enable Exchange routing functionality.
IPSec Services	Automatic	This service provides end-to-end security between clients and servers on TCP/IP networks and should be enabled to provide an Internet Protocol security (IPSec) filter on OWA servers.
IIS Admin Service	Automatic	This service is dependent on the MSExchange routing engine and must be enabled to allow Exchange routing functionality.
World Wide Web Publishing Service	Automatic	This service must be enabled for client computers to communicate with OWA or OMA front-end servers.
Exchange IMAP4	Disabled	This service is not required unless the server is also configured as the front-end server for Internet Message Access Protocol version 4rev1 (IMAP4) clients.
Exchange store	Disabled	This service is only required if there are user mailboxes or public folders; it is disabled because front-end servers do not contain user data.
Exchange POP3	Disabled	This service is not required unless the server is also configured as the front-end server for Post Office Protocol version 3 (POP3) clients.
Microsoft Search Service	Disabled	This service is only used for full-text indexing of information stores; it is disabled because front-end servers do not contain user data.
Microsoft Exchange Event Service	Disabled	This service is only required for compatibility with previous versions of Exchange.
Microsoft Exchange Site Replication Service	Disabled	This service is only required for compatibility with previous versions of Exchange.
Exchange System Manager	Disabled	This service can be disabled if you do not require message tracking to audit message flow through Exchange.

(continued)

Service name	Startup mode	Reason
Microsoft Exchange MTA Stacks	Disabled	This service is only required for compatibility with previous versions of Exchange or if there are X.400 connectors.
RPC Locator	Disabled	This service is no longer required for communication with a domain controller or for the System Attendant to start.
SMTP	Disabled	Outlook Web Access does not require SMTP to be configured on the front-end server; it can be disabled unless this server is also used as a SMTP server. If the server will also be an SMTP server, the information store and System Attendant services are also required.
NNTP	Disabled	This service (Network News Transfer Protocol) is only required for installation and if newsgroup functionality is required.

Additional service considerations are as follows:

- *Exchange System Attendant.* System Attendant can be disabled and is only required on a front-end server if you intend to make configuration changes to Exchange. Before stopping this service, ensure that all configuration changes are complete.

- *Exchange System Manager.* The service allows you to specify, through the user interface (UI), which domain controller or global catalog server Exchange 2003 will use when accessing the directory. This service is also required for message tracking. You can disable this service without affecting the core functionality of Exchange. However, you may need message tracking to troubleshoot message delivery.

Secure IIS

OWA and OMA require IIS, so you need to ensure that IIS is secure before deploying the front-end server. You can use utilities such as the IIS Lockdown Tool and URLScan Security Tool to secure your OWA servers. For more information about securing IIS, see the Security Tools and Checklists page of the Microsoft TechNet Web site at http://www.microsoft.com/technet/treeview/. Also, search for the article "XCCC: IIS Lockdown and URLscan Configurations in an Exchange Environment" on the Product Support Services page of the Microsoft Web site at http://support.microsoft.com/.

Secure traffic from the screened subnet to the internal network

A front-end server only can use port 80 to communicate with a back-end server; therefore, it cannot use SSL encryption. To secure the communication between the front-end and back-end servers, configure an IPSec policy that will force the encryption of the network traffic. You can configure an IPSec policy that will encrypt all traffic between the front-end and back-end servers, or you can configure the policy to encrypt only selected traffic. For example, if a front-end server uses Kerberos to authenticate users, all authentication traffic between the front-end server and the domain controllers is already secure. At a minimum, the IPSec policy should require the encryption of all HTTP traffic (port 80).

Impact of Virus and Content Scanners on Messaging Functionality

One of the more difficult components to troubleshoot in messaging is third-party scanning software. Messages need to be scanned in order to stop virus infections and the propagation of virus infections to other e-mail systems on the Internet.

Over the past couple of years, companies have started to realize that their e-mail servers are being clogged with non-business related e-mail (e.g., personal e-mail between friends), Unsolicited Commercial E-mail (UCE; also known as spam), and even e-mail that is meant to maliciously harm the company.

Virus Infections

Virus infections are bad news for a number of reasons:

- Lost productivity of end-users
- Poor server performance (the Melissa virus is a great example)
- Unable to process important business messages
- Spreading the virus to other companies can cause a temporary e-mail block
- Publicity that impacts the stock value of a company

To prevent virus infections, antivirus software must be kept up to date. Antivirus software usually exists in several places in a company, including:

- *Firewalls or viruswalls*. Firewalls and viruswalls can be troublesome as many of them do not support all of the SMTP verbs available and may cause problems depending on the origination system and the type of message being sent.
- *E-mail servers*. Most antivirus software packages will scan the stores on a regular basis and will scan all new messages as they arrive.
- *File servers*. Users often pull attachments from file servers, so it is good to know that they will be virus free before they are sent.
- *Client computers*. In the event a virus gets past any of the other antivirus applications, you need to be aware that a client-side antivirus application may end up deleting messages through the Outlook client.

Content Scanning

Content scanning is not just looking for virus infected files. Content scanning is utilized by many companies to:

- Combat SPAM.
- Keep users from sending proprietary information outside the company.
- Keep users from sending explicit e-mails to others.
- Keep outside e-mail that may lead to sexual harassment concerns from being sent to users.

The problem that occurs most often with content scanning is that many false positives can occur, leading to lost productivity and a great deal of administrative effort to fix the scanning solution.

Performance Impact   While it is acknowledged that virus and content scanners are needed in many cases, the related performance decreases can be very significant. You might need to install extra CPUs and RAM to handle the load placed on your e-mail server by these scanners.

Administrative Impact   You also need to be aware that positive scanner hits, as well as false positive hits, will mean that some messages are being lost. Some users will assume something is wrong with the e-mail server when they do not get the e-mails that they are expecting, and this can lead to extra, unnecessary troubleshooting work since there is not a problem with your e-mail server. Be ready to check quarantine logs for messages as part of the troubleshooting process for lost messages.

Using the Telnet Command to Test the TCP Port Restrictions on a Firewall

If you feel that the firewall might be the source of a problem, you can use Telnet to test the firewall port restrictions. From inside the firewall to the Internet, you will need to find a server that will accept your session. For example, if you want to test whether SMTP is open and allowing traffic from inside the network to outside the network, you will need to have a target system somewhere outside the firewall that will accept SMTP commands. Basically, this is any e-mail server on the Internet. To test SMTP, use the following steps:

Test SMTP – Port 25

1. Click **Start**, click **Run**, type **CMD** and then click **OK**.

2. At the command prompt, type **telnet** *company.com* **25** (where *company.com* is the domain name of the e-mail server) and wait for the response.

   If the target is an Exchange Server 2003 server with a properly configured MX record and the firewall allows port 25 traffic outside the company, you will receive the following message:

   220 *company.com* (where *company.com* is the domain name of the e-mail server) Microsoft ESMTP MAIL Service, Version: 6.0.3790.0 ready at Sun, 10 Aug 2003 04:08:26 -0600

3. Type **quit** at the prompt to close the connection.

You can use this same procedure from outside the company to test the firewall and make sure port 25 is open to allow incoming e-mail traffic.

Test POP3 – Port 110 and 995

Generally, you will only allow remote network users to access Exchange Server 2003 using POP3, since internal clients will be better served using the Outlook client. To test from outside the firewall, use the following steps:

1. Click **Start**, click **Run**, type **CMD** and then click **OK**.

2. At the command prompt, type **telnet** *company.com* **110** (where *company.com* is the domain name of the e-mail server) and wait for the response.

   If the target is an Exchange Server 2003 server and the firewall allows port 110 traffic from outside the company, you will receive the following message:

   +OK Microsoft Exchange Server 2003 POP3 server version 6.5.6944.0 *company.com* (where *company.com* is the domain name of the e-mail server) ready

3. Type **quit** at the prompt to close the connection.

4. Test 995, which is used for SSL-protected POP3 services, using the same process, but typing **995** instead of 110.

Test IMAP4 – Port 143 and 993

Generally, you will only allow remote network users to access Exchange Server 2003 using IMAP4, since internal clients will be better served using the Outlook client. To test from outside of the firewall, use the following steps:

1. Click **Start**, click **Run**, type **CMD** and then click **OK**.

2. At the command prompt, type **telnet** *company.com* **143** (where *company.com* is the domain name of the e-mail server) and wait for the response.

   If the target is an Exchange 2003 server and the firewall allows port 143 traffic from outside the company, you will receive the following message:

   * OK Microsoft Exchange Server 2003 IMAP4rev1 server version 6.5.6944.0 *company.com* (where *company.com* is the domain name of the e-mail server) ready

3. Type **IMAP Logout** at the prompt to close the connection.

4. Test 993, which is used for SSL-protected IMAP4 services, using the same process, typing **993** instead of 143.

Other ports

You can use Telnet to test the firewall to see if other ports are open and verify that the server responds to the traffic type used by the port. For example, you can test NNTP port availability to use port number 119. Once connected, you can send NNTP commands and verify that NNTP is functioning as expected.

Verifying That a Server is Online

During troubleshooting, you may need to verify remotely that a server is online. This verification can include several steps. In most cases, you should start by verifying basic network connectivity, then verify name resolution, and then verify service availability.

1. To verify network connectivity, ping the IP address of the remote server. If the ping is successful, move on to the next step in troubleshooting. If the ping is not successful, determine whether there is a network failure by pinging another server in the same subnet, or by using **pathping** or **tracert** to determine where the failure occurs.

2. If the ping is successful, ping the fully qualified domain name of the server. If the ping is successful, move on to the next step. If the ping is not successful, use tools such as NSLookup or DNSLint to determine the DNS zone information and server configuration. You may also need to check the Hosts file; in most cases the Hosts file should not contain any information.

3. In some cases, clients may need to connect to the server using network basic input/output system (NetBIOS) names. This is true if you have older clients such as Microsoft Windows 95, Microsoft Windows 98, or Microsoft Windows NT® workstations on your network. To verify NetBIOS connectivity, use the **Net Use** command, or use Netdiag.exe. You can also use the **Browstat.exe** command (included in the Windows Server 2003 Support Tools) to perform detailed troubleshooting of NetBIOS browser troubleshooting.

4. If you can successfully connect to the server using host and NetBIOS names, the next step in troubleshooting is to test protocol connectivity. The best tool to test e-mail-related protocol connectivity is Telnet. If you cannot connect to the server using Telnet, verify that the required protocol is not blocked by a network device.

5. If you cannot connect to the server using Telnet, confirm that the required services are running on the Exchange server. The services that must be running on a front-end server are discussed in Securing a Front-End and Back-End Server Infrastructure in this Toolkit resource.

   The following services must be running on a back-end server:

   - Exchange System Attendant

   - Exchange store

   - Exchange System Manager

   - Windows Management Instrumentation

   - Microsoft Exchange Routing Engine

   - IIS Admin Service

   - SMTP

   - World Wide Web Publishing Service

   - Additional services, like NNTP, Exchange IMAP4, Exchange POP3, HTTP SSL Microsoft Exchange Event Service, Microsoft Exchange Site Replication Service, and Microsoft Exchange MTA Stacks, may be required to support Internet protocol clients or for compatibility with previous versions of Exchange.

Note   These services are dependent on Windows Server 2003 services. View the properties of each service to confirm the service dependencies.

To verify the status of the services on a remote computer, you can connect to the computer using a custom Computer Management Microsoft Management Console (MMC) or Remote Desktop. If the required services are functional on the server, verify that the Exchange mailbox and public folder stores are mounted. You can use the Exchange System Manager to verify the mounted stores.

Verifying the Configuration of the Default Web Site

By default, OWA is configured to use the default Web site on an Exchange Server. Other than configuring the Web site for SSL, you should not modify it.

Note   If you want to use a Web site other than the default web site for OWA, you must create the Web site using the Exchange System Manager. You can also create additional virtual directories using the Exchange System Manager. You will need to do this if you are enabling OWA access for DNS domains in addition to the default domain specified in the default recipient policy.

Default Web site configuration

You can view and configure some of the default Web site properties using either Exchange System Manager or IIS Manager.

When IIS 6.0 is installed on a computer running Windows Server 2003, the server is restricted to only providing static HTML content. If you want to enable other types of content such as .asp pages, you must enable this Web extension. When you install Exchange Server 2003 on a Windows Server 2003 server, some of the Web extensions are enabled by default. The following figure shows the default configuration.

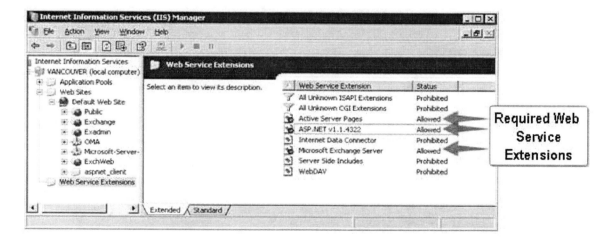

When an Exchange server is configured to support OWA and OMA, the virtual directories shown in the following figure are configured under the default Web site.

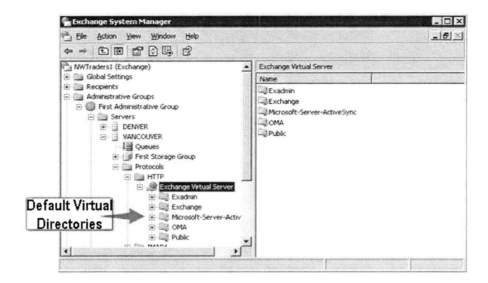

The default permissions and authentication settings for the Exchange virtual directory are shown below.

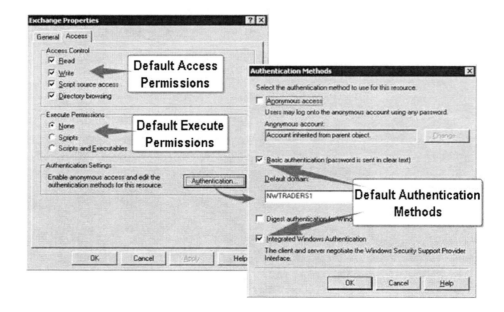

Configuring OWA for SSL

By default, the Exchange virtual directory is not enabled for SSL. In order to configure SSL, you must follow this procedure:

1. Install a Web server certificate on the Exchange server. If you are using the default Web site, open Internet Information Services (IIS) Manager and click the **Directory Security** tab on the Web site properties.

2. Under **Secure Communications**, click **Server Certificate**. The IIS Certificate Wizard will start. Fill in the requested information and then submit the certificate request to a Certificate Authority (CA). You can submit the request to an online CA or create a file to be sent to an offline CA.

3. If you sent the request to an online CA, the certificate is automatically installed on the server. If you sent the request to an offline CA, you must restart the IIS Certificate Wizard after you receive the certificate and install the certificate on the server.

4. Configure the Exchange virtual directory in Internet Information Services (IIS) Manager to use the server certificate for SSL.

5. To enable SSL, access the Exchange virtual directory properties and click the **Directory Security** tab. Under **Secure Communications**, click **Edit**. You can choose to require SSL; require, accept, or ignore client certificates; and configure certificate mapping to user accounts.

Unit 5: Troubleshooting Client Connectivity

E-Mail Blocked from Subscribers of an Exclusion List (Block List)

E-mail can be blocked by recipient Simple Mail Transfer Protcol (SMTP) servers for a number of reasons. One reason is that some SMTP servers will allow anyone to send e-mail to the Internet without authentication and without restraints. These servers are referred to as Open Relay SMTP servers. Lists of these open relay SMTP servers (called *exclusion lists* or *block lists*) are kept by a few different groups and are sold or provided for no fee to subscribers.

How do I know if I am on a list?

If your company mail server is on a block list, e-mail will bounce back to your users if the receiving company subscribes to one of the lists. The e-mail returned to your users will also provide information about which list your company is on and how to remove your company from the list.

Why do these lists exist?

Unsolicited Commercial E-mail (UCE) is also known as *spam*. Spam is a major problem in our industry because it costs companies extra resources to process additional messages and costs e-mail users considerable time to manage these additional messages.

One way to fight spam is to block the IP addresses and domain names of companies that allow spam to be sent. An even tougher way to prevent spam is to install content filtering software.

The companies and individuals that send spam know that their IP addresses and domain names are blocked, so they search the Internet for unsuspecting companies' SMTP servers that they can bounce e-mail off of, making it appear as if the spam came from those servers instead of the spammer.

Avoiding block lists

To avoid being put on one of these lists, you need to make sure that your SMTP servers are not configured as open relay SMTP servers. To verify this, check the properties of your local SMTP virtual servers.

This is more difficult than it first appears. There may be several SMTP servers installed in your company that were not approved. You should use a port scanner to search your network for any systems that have port 25 open.

It is likely that you are using a non-authorized SMTP server to avoid content filtering or to avoid it being tracked and monitored in the Microsoft® Exchange Server 2003 environment. In most cases, the only way these SMTP servers can be used as an open relay would be if the firewall allowed incoming SMTP traffic to them, and this is unlikely for a larger organization. However, remember that in Microsoft Windows® 2000 SMTP was installed by default when installing Internet Information Services (IIS), so it is possible that your company Web servers can be used as open relays.

Check the Exchange Server 2003 environment

By using the Exchange Server 2003 Help files, you can easily check the configuration of the SMTP virtual servers to make sure they don't allow anonymous authentication. Pay special attention to any front-end servers in your company and any servers that are accessible from the Internet.

Fixing block listings

At your request, organizations that maintain block lists may re-test your SMTP servers and remove your servers from the list. Most of these organizations will also provide detailed step-by-step instructions on how to make sure your SMTP servers do not allow open relaying of UCE.

Smart Hosts

What is a smart host?

A *smart host* is a SMTP server that is used by a company to send e-mail to the Internet.

Why do we use smart hosts?

A smart host allows messages to be sent over a connection that is more direct or less costly than other routes. Smart hosts also allow the installation of scanning software, such as antivirus and content scanning software, in one place. If all e-mail is directed through a smart host, you can be sure that it is properly scanned before it is sent to the Internet.

How do I verify that I am using a smart host?

To verify that your Exchange Server 2003 server is using a smart host, open Exchange System Manager and follow these steps:

1. Click **Start**, **All Programs**, **Microsoft Exchange**, and then **System Manager**.

2. Expand the Servers node, the Server name, the Protocols node, and then SMTP.

3. Right-click the **SMTP Virtual Server** and click **Properties**.

4. Click the **Delivery** tab and click the **Advanced** button.

5. If present, the smart host name or IP address will appear in the Smart Host field.

Note   Multiple smart hosts can be entered in this field if they are separated by commas or semi-colons.

How do I verify that a smart host is running?

Verifying that a Smart Host is running is the same thing as verifying that a SMTP server is running on any particular machine. Follow these steps:

1. Open a command prompt, type **Telnet smarthost 25** and press ENTER.

2. If the smart host is running Exchange Server 2003, it will respond: as shown below (the date and time will be current):

220 smarthost.company.com Microsoft ESMTP MAIL Service, Version: 6.0.3790.0 ready at Sun, 10 Aug 2003 04:08:26 -0600

Using the Telnet Command to Test the TCP Port Restrictions on a Firewall

If you feel that the firewall might be the source of a problem, you can use Telnet to test the firewall port restrictions. From inside the firewall to the Internet, you will need to find a server that will accept your session. For example, if you want to test whether SMTP is open and allowing traffic from inside the network to outside the network, you will need to have a target system somewhere outside the firewall that will accept SMTP commands. Basically, this is any e-mail server on the Internet. To test SMTP, follow these steps:

Test SMTP – Port 25

1. Click **Start**, click **Run**, type **CMD** and then click **OK**.

2. At the command prompt, type **telnet** *company.com* **25** (where *company.com* is the domain name of the e-mail server) and wait for the response.

   If the target is an Exchange Server 2003 server with a properly configured MX record and the firewall allows port 25 traffic outside the company, you will receive the following message:

   220 *company.com* (where *company.com* is the domain name of the e-mail server) Microsoft ESMTP MAIL Service, Version: 6.0.3790.0 ready at Sun, 10 Aug 2003 04:08:26 -0600

3. Type **quit** at the prompt to close the connection.

You can use this same procedure from outside the company to test the firewall and make sure port 25 is open to allow incoming e-mail traffic.

Test POP3 – Port 110 and 995

Generally, you will only allow remote network users to access Exchange Server 2003 using Post Office Protocol version 3 (POP3), since internal clients will be better served using the Outlook client. To test from outside the firewall, use the following steps:

1. Click **Start**, click **Run**, type **CMD** and then click **OK**.

2. At the command prompt, type **telnet** *company.com* **110** (where *company.com* is the domain name of the e-mail server) and wait for the response.

   If the target is an Exchange Server 2003 server and the firewall allows port 110 traffic from outside the company, you will receive the following message:

   +OK Microsoft Exchange Server 2003 POP3 server version 6.5.6944.0 *company.com* (where *company.com* is the domain name of the e-mail server) ready

3. Type **quit** at the prompt to close the connection.

4. Test 995, which is used for Secure Sockets Layer- (SSL) protected POP3 services, using the same process, but typing **995** instead of 110.

Test IMAP4 – Port 143 and 993

Generally, you will only allow remote network users to access Exchange Server 2003 using Internet Message Access Protocol version 4rev1 (IMAP4), since internal clients will be better served using the Outlook client. To test from outside the firewall, use the following steps:

1. Click **Start**, click **Run**, type **CMD** and then click **OK**.

2. At the command prompt, type **telnet** *company.com* **143** (where *company.com* is the domain name of the e-mail server) and wait for the response.

   If the target is an Exchange 2003 server and the firewall allows port 143 traffic from outside the company, you will receive the following message:

   * OK Microsoft Exchange Server 2003 IMAP4rev1 server version 6.5.6944.0 *company.com* (where *company.com* is the domain name of the e-mail server) ready

3. Type **IMAP Logout** at the prompt to close the connection.

4. Test 993, which is used for SSL-protected IMAP4 services, using the same process, typing **993** instead of 143.

Other ports

You can use Telnet to test the firewall to see if other ports are open and verify that the server responds to the traffic type used by the port. For example, you can test Network News Transfer Protocol (NNTP) port availability to use port number 119. Once connected, you can send NNTP commands and verify that NNTP is functioning as expected.

Verifying That a Server Is Online

During troubleshooting, you may need to verify remotely that a server is online. This verification can include several steps. In most cases, you should start by verifying basic network connectivity, then verify name resolution, and then verify service availability.

1. To verify network connectivity, ping the IP address of the remote server. If the ping is successful, move on to the next step in troubleshooting. If the ping is not successful, determine whether there is a network failure by pinging another server in the same subnet, or by using **pathping** or **tracert** to determine where the failure occurs.

2. If the ping is successful, ping the fully qualified domain name of the server. If the ping is successful, move on to the next step. If the ping is not successful, use tools such as NSLookup or DNSLint to determine the DNS zone information and server configuration. You may also need to check the Hosts file; in most cases, the Hosts file should not contain any information.

3. In some cases, clients may need to connect to the server using network basic input/output system (NetBIOS) names. This is true if you have older clients such as Microsoft Windows 95, Microsoft Windows 98, or Microsoft Windows NT® workstations on your network. To verify NetBIOS connectivity, use the **Net Use** command, or use Netdiag.exe. You can also use the **Browstat.exe** command (included in the Windows Server 2003 Support Tools) to perform detailed NetBIOS browser troubleshooting.

4. If you can successfully connect to the server using host and NetBIOS names, the next step in troubleshooting is to test protocol connectivity. The best tool to test e-mail-related protocol connectivity is Telnet. If you cannot connect to the server using Telnet, verify that the required protocol is not blocked by a network device.

5. If you cannot connect to the server using Telnet, confirm that the required services are running on the Exchange server. The services that must be running on a front-end server are discussed in Securing a Front-End and Back-End Server Infrastructure in this Toolkit resource.

   The following services must be running on a back-end server:

   - Exchange System Attendant
   - Exchange store
   - Exchange System Manager
   - Windows Management Instrumentation
   - Microsoft Exchange Routing Engine
   - IIS Admin Service
   - SMTP
   - World Wide Web Publishing Service
   - Additional services, like NNTP, Exchange IMAP4, Exchange POP3, HTTP SSL Microsoft Exchange Event Service, Microsoft Exchange Site Replication Service, and Microsoft Exchange MTA Stacks, may be required to support Internet protocol clients or for compatibility with previous versions of Exchange.

Note These services are dependent on Windows Server™ 2003 services. View the properties of each service to confirm the service dependencies.

To verify the status of the services on a remote computer, you can connect to the computer using a custom Computer Management Microsoft Management Console (MMC) or Remote Desktop. If the required services are functional on the server, verify that the Exchange mailbox and public folder stores are mounted. You can use the Exchange System Manager to verify the mounted stores.

Impact of Virus and Content Scanners on Messaging Functionality

One of the more difficult components to troubleshoot in messaging is third-party scanning software. Messages need to be scanned in order to stop virus infections and the propagation of virus infections to other e-mail systems on the Internet.

Over the past couple of years, companies have started to realize that their e-mail servers are being clogged with non-business related e-mail (e.g., personal e-mail between friends), Unsolicited Commercial E-mail (UCE; also known as spam), and even e-mail that is meant to maliciously harm the company.

Virus infections

Virus infections are bad news for a number of reasons:

- Lost productivity of end-users
- Poor server performance (the Melissa virus is a great example)
- Unable to process our important business messages
- Spreading the virus to other companies can cause a temporary e-mail block
- Publicity that impacts the stock value of a company

To prevent virus infections, antivirus software must be kept up to date. Antivirus software usually exists in several places in a company, including:

- *Firewalls or viruswalls.* Firewalls and viruswalls can be troublesome as many of them do not support all of the SMTP verbs available and may cause problems depending on the origination system and the type of message being sent.
- *E-mail servers.* Most antivirus software packages will scan the stores on a regular basis and will scan all new messages as they arrive.
- *File servers.* Users often pull attachments from file servers, so it is good to know that they will be virus free before they are sent.
- *Client computers.* In the event a virus gets past any of the other antivirus applications, you need to be aware that a client-side antivirus application may end up deleting messages through the Microsoft Outlook® client.

Content scanning

Content scanning is not just looking for virus infected files. Content scanning is utilized by many companies to:

- Combat spam.
- Keep users from sending proprietary information outside the company.
- Keep users from sending explicit e-mails to others.
- Keep outside e-mail that may lead to sexual harassment concerns from being sent to users.

The problem that occurs most often with content scanning is that many false positives can occur, leading to lost productivity and a great deal of administrative effort to fix the scanning solution.

Performance impact   While it is acknowledged that virus and content scanners are needed in many cases, the related performance decreases can be very significant. You might need to install extra CPUs and RAM to handle the load placed on your e-mail server by these scanners.

Administrative impact   Also, you need to be aware that positive scanner hits, as well as false positive hits, will mean that some messages are lost. Some users will assume something is wrong with the e-mail server when they do not get the e-mails that they are expecting, and this can lead to extra, unnecessary troubleshooting work since there is not a problem with your e-mail server. Be ready to check quarantine logs for messages as part of the troubleshooting process for lost messages.

Unit 6: Troubleshooting Server Connectivity

Checking Global Settings

Global settings are used to configure default e-mail settings that apply to your entire organization. When troubleshooting e-mail delivery problems, you should verify that messages are not being blocked because of the global settings. Many of the global settings can be modified and overwritten by configuration settings on other objects in a Microsoft® Exchange Server 2003 organization.

Configuring Internet message formats

You can configure the default settings for e-mail messages delivered to other organizations using the Internet Message Format option. The default Internet Message Format setting applies to all Simple Mail Transfer Protocol (SMTP) messages sent outside your organization. You can configure additional message formats that will affect how messages will be delivered to specific destination domains.

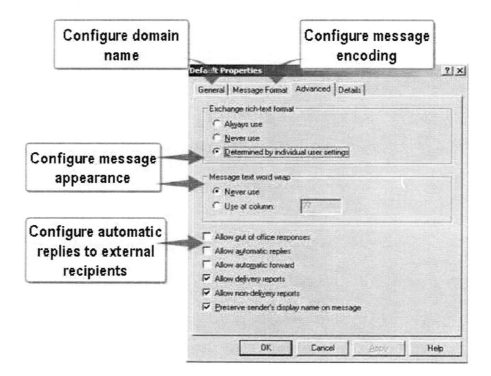

To configure the Internet Message Format option, follow these steps:

1.   Right-click **Internet Message Format**, click **New**, and then click **Domain**.

2.   Type a name for the new object and then type the name of the SMTP domain.

3.   Configure the message formats for the specific domain. You can modify the domain name on the **General** tab.

You can also configure the default message encoding to be applied to all messages. To configure the default message encoding, click the **Message Format** tab, and click **UUEncode** or **MIME** and configure the encoding options.

You can configure message appearance and automatic replies on the **Advanced** tab. The interface is shown above.

Configuring message delivery

You can also configure global settings for message delivery that will be applied to all messages sent to or from your organization by using the following two options:

- *Defaults tab*. Use this tab to configure default message size limits and recipient limits. These limits can be overwritten by limits set on objects such as SMTP connectors or mailboxes.

- *Filtering tab*. Use this tab to configure block lists. *Block lists* are used to block connections from external SMTP servers based on DNS domain names or IP addresses. You can also configure sender and recipient block lists to block e-mail messages from specific senders or to block e-mail being sent to specific recipients.

  - When you configure block lists on the **Filtering** tab, you must apply the filter to the appropriate SMTP virtual server. To do this, access the SMTP virtual server properties in Exchange System Manager. Click **Advanced** and then click **Select** to apply the appropriate filters.

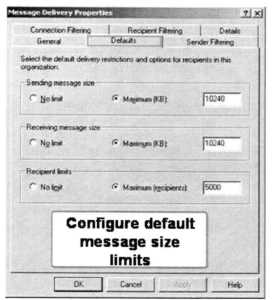

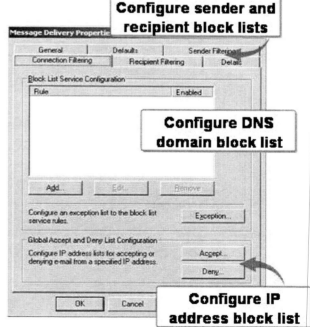

Identifying and Closing Open Relays

A server configured for open relaying will accept SMTP messages from any SMTP domain and forward the message to any other SMTP domain. If your server is configured this way, an unauthorized user can send a single e-mail message with multiple recipients to your SMTP server and your server will forward the message to all the recipients. Users that send out Unsolicited Commercial E-mail (UCE), or spam, might use your server to send these messages.

If your server is configured for open relaying, you may experience performance problems, since your server could be sending thousands of e-mails. If your SMTP queue is growing rapidly or if you notice a significant increase in SMTP traffic, check your server for open relaying.

In addition, if your company has an open relay SMTP server, your company may also be put on a block list. Many companies use block lists to prevent connections from servers that are known for forwarding UCE. Companies may add your SMTP server to an internal list of open relay servers or they may subscribe to a block list that is maintained by a third-party company, such as Mail Abuse Prevention System (MAPS). (Block lists that are maintained by third-party companies are typically called Realtime Blackhole Lists or Relay Blocking Lists.) If your server does appear on the block list of a third-party company, companies that subscribe to the list will block all connections from your SMTP server.

Testing for open relays using Telnet

You can use Telnet to test whether your server is configured for open relaying. To test this, use a computer that is connected to the Internet and follow this procedure:

1. Open a command prompt and type **Telnet** *smtpservername* **25** (where *smtpservername* is the name of the specific SMTP server). The destination server will respond with a series of 250 commands.

2. Type **Mail from:** *user@domain.com* (where *user@domain.com* is a dummy account with a domain name different than your internal domain name).

3. The server should respond with "250 2.1.0 user@domain.com Sender OK."

4. Type **Rcpt to:** *user2@domain2.com* (where *user2@domain2.com* is a dummy account with a domain name different than your internal domain name).

If your server responds with "250 2.1.5 user2@domain2.com," it is configured for an open relaying. If your server responds with "550 5.7.1 Unable to relay for domain2.com," it is not relaying for that domain.

Closing open relays

Information on closing open relays in Exchange Server 2003 is located in Exchange Help. To locate the information, open Exchange System Manager, click **Help**, click **Help Topics**, and then click **Search**. Search for **Set Relay Restrictions** and then click the topic "**Set Relay Restrictions on Virtual Servers**."

Using Dcdiag and Netdiag to Verify the Network Infrastructure

The DCDiag command   DCDiag will perform the following:

- Verify that the domain can support Microsoft Active Directory®.
- Determine if it is possible to create an Active Directory forest.
- Determine if it is possible to add another domain controller to an existing domain.
- Determine if a Microsoft Windows® 2000, Microsoft Windows XP, or Microsoft Windows Server™ 2003 computer can be added to the domain.
- Test replication between domain controllers.
- Report down servers.
- Test that all domain controllers are advertising their presence to other domain controllers.

DCDiag can be used to test the state of domain controllers in a forest. It will report any problems it finds.

/v   Verbose mode will provide more information in an easier-to-read format. The /v switch will also provide information about the Flexible Single Master Operation (FSMO) roles.

/f   The /f switch is used to point to a file for logging the results of the DCDiag command.

/?   The help switch will provide more information about the other options that are available for the DCDiag command.

The NetDiag command   NetDiag tests network connectivity by testing the following items:

- Network adapter interface information, including the:
  - Host name
  - IP address
  - Subnet mask
  - Default gateway
  - DNS server
  - Windows Internet Name Service (WINS) server
- Domain membership
- Loopback ping test
- Default gateway ping test
- Network basic input/output system (NetBIOS) name check
- Winsock test
- DNS test
- Domain controller discovery test
- Trust relationship test
- Lightweight Directory Access Protocol (LDAP) test
- Internet Protocol Security (IPSec) test

/v   The tests performed by NetDiag will alert you to many possible problems. You can expand on the result messages by using the /v switch to turn on verbose mode.

/l   The tests performed by NetDiag can result in a large amount of output. It may also be necessary to send the resulting information to others to review. Using the /l switch will capture the information to a log file in the same directory as the netdiag.exe file.

/?   The help switch will provide more information about the other options that are available for the NetDiag command.

Using WinRoute to Troubleshoot Routing

WinRoute is a useful tool for monitoring and troubleshooting message routing problems in Exchange Server 2003. WinRoute provides you with detailed information about the routing configuration in your Exchange organization, as well as information about which links are available.

WinRoute is not included in a standard installation of Exchange Server 2003. You can download the tool from the Microsoft Exchange Web site at http://www.microsoft.com/exchange/tools.

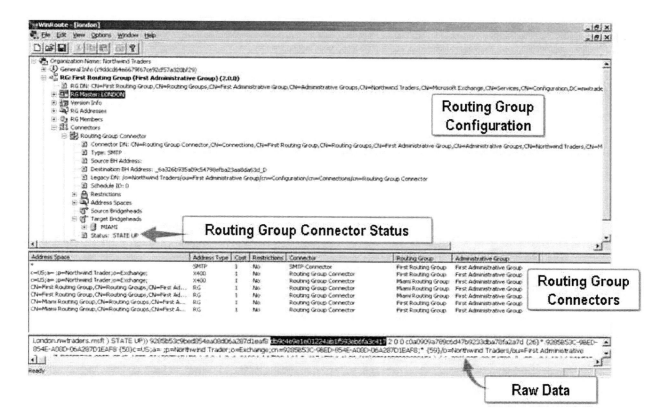

To use Winroute, follow these steps:

1. Download the WinRoute tool and copy it to your workstation or server. Open a Run command and start WinRoute.exe.

2. To collect information about the routing configuration in your Exchange organization, click **File** and then click **New Query**. Type the name of the Exchange server that you want to query and click **OK**.

WinRoute displays the routing groups and routing group connector information for the entire organization. View this information to determine the configuration and status of routing group connectors and other connectors. The raw data pane contains actual information extracted from Active Directory and also is useful for locating other information, such as server or routing group connector GUIDs.

Verifying That a Server Is Online

During troubleshooting, you may need to verify remotely that a server is online. This verification can include several steps. In most cases, you should start by verifying basic network connectivity, then verify name resolution, and then verify service availability.

1. To verify network connectivity, ping the IP address of the remote server. If the ping is successful, move on to the next step in troubleshooting. If the ping is not successful, determine whether there is a network failure by pinging another server in the same subnet, or by using **pathping** or **tracert** to determine where the failure occurs.

2. If the ping is successful, ping the fully qualified domain name of the server. If the ping is successful, move on to the next step. If the ping is not successful, use tools such as NSLookup or DNSLint to determine the DNS zone information and server configuration. You may also need to check the Hosts file; in most cases, the Hosts file should not contain any information.

3. In some cases, clients may need to connect to the server using NetBIOS names. This is true if you have older clients such as Microsoft Windows 95, Microsoft Windows 98, or Microsoft Windows NT® workstations on your network. To verify NetBIOS connectivity, use the **Net Use** command, or use Netdiag.exe. You can also use the **Browstat.exe** command (included in the Windows Server 2003 Support Tools) to perform detailed NetBIOS browser troubleshooting.

4. If you can successfully connect to the server using host and NetBIOS names, the next step in troubleshooting is to test protocol connectivity. The best tool to test e-mail-related protocol connectivity is Telnet. If you cannot connect to the server using Telnet, verify that the required protocol is not blocked by a network device.

5. If you cannot connect to the server using Telnet, confirm that the required services are running on the Exchange server. The services that must be running on a front-end server are discussed in Securing a Front-End and Back-End Server Infrastructure in this Toolkit resource.

   The following services must be running on a back-end server:

   - Exchange System Attendant
   - Exchange store
   - Exchange System Manager
   - Windows Management Instrumentation
   - Microsoft Exchange Routing Engine
   - Internet Information Services (IIS) Admin Service
   - SMTP
   - World Wide Web Publishing Service
   - Additional services, like Network News Transfer Protocol (NNTP), Exchange Internet Access Message Protocol version 4rev1 (IMAP4), Exchange Post Office Protocol version 3 (POP3), HTTP SSL Microsoft Exchange Event Service, Microsoft Exchange Site Replication Service, and Microsoft Exchange MTA Stacks, may be required to support Internet protocol clients or for compatibility with previous versions of Exchange.

Note These services are dependent on Windows Server 2003 services. View the properties of each service to confirm the service dependencies.

To verify the status of the services on a remote computer, you can connect to the computer using a custom Computer Management Microsoft Management Console (MMC) or Remote Desktop. If the required services are functional on the server, verify that the Exchange mailbox and public folder stores are mounted. You can use the Exchange System Manager to verify the mounted stores.

Viewing Delivery Restrictions on SMTP Connectors

One reason why a user cannot send and receive Internet e-mail may be the delivery restrictions on the SMTP connector that is used to send and receive e-mail from the Internet. These delivery restrictions can be used to limit which users can send e-mail using the SMTP connector, and therefore can restrict users from sending e-mail to the Internet. The SMTP connector can also be configured to limit the size of messages that can be sent using the connector. This size limitation applies to messages sent in both directions on the SMTP connector.

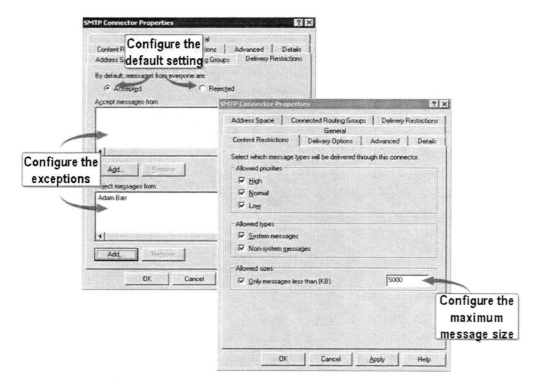

To view the properties of an SMTP connector, follow this procedure:

1. In Exchange System Manager, expand the Administrative Groups container and then expand the specific administrative group.

2. Expand the Routing Groups container, and then expand the specific routing group.

3. Expand the Connectors container. Right-click the **SMTP connector** and click **Properties**.

4. The **Delivery Restrictions** tab is used to limit who can send e-mail using this connector. You must first identify the default setting for the connector by determining if messages sent by everyone are accepted (allowed) or rejected (not allowed). Then you can configure the exceptions to the default rule. For example, if you allow everyone to use the connector, you need to configure those accounts that should not be allowed to send mail using the connector.

5. The **Content Restrictions** tab is used to configure the maximum message size that can be sent using the connector. To enable this, you must select **Only messages less than (KB)** and then specify a maximum message size.

Unit 7: Troubleshooting Server Performance

Antivirus Scanning for Exchange

E-mail can include infected HTML code, infected scripts, and other infected files. Microsoft® Exchange Server 2003 includes an antivirus application programming interface (API) that can be used by antivirus vendors to scan e-mail as it enters an Exchange server and as it leaves an Exchange server. Antivirus vendors also include the ability to completely scan mailbox and public folder stores on a regular basis, just in case the antivirus solution was offline, not fully updated, or had been previously infected.

What should I do?

As an Exchange administrator, you need to keep on top of all Microsoft Windows Server™ 2003 fixes, all Exchange Server 2003 fixes, and all updates to your company's antivirus software. Failure to protect the messaging environment can mean catastrophic loss of messaging data that is vital to the organization.

Keep antivirus software updated

You need to remember that antivirus software includes several pieces that need to be kept updated:

- *The antivirus software itself.* Many antivirus software vendors release new versions that have better performance or have been updated to include new features. It is very important to have a current version of your company's antivirus software.

- *The antivirus engine.* Most antivirus software vendors will update their engine in response to new technology used in virus attacks and to improve scanning performance. The engine is a key portion of the software because even if you have the rest of your solution updated, an out-of-date engine can prevent your solution from identifying virus infections.

- *The antivirus signature list.* This antivirus software file is often referred to as the *signature file* or the *.dat file* (many vendors use the .dat extension to identify this file). This file contains the information used by the engine during the scanning process to identify possible infections.

Test

Although it may seem like basic business sense, it is clear that many companies do not test changes to their Exchange server environment. Updating antivirus software should require some testing, even if it is minimal. It is not likely that an update to the antivirus solution will cause messaging failures, but it is possible. As with any highly visible application with such importance to a business, Exchange server updates of all kinds should be tested.

Use quarantine features

All antivirus software includes the ability to quarantine files that it identifies as infected or possibly infected or just delete them. It is a very good practice to use the quarantine feature for two reasons.

First, the quarantine feature saves troubleshooting effort in many situations. Users often complain about a message that was not received from a friend or business associate. It is very helpful to be able to refer to the quarantine directory and see if the message in question was removed because of an infection.

Secondly, using the quarantine feature will allow you to identify the source of many virus infections. You can then take action to let your peers at other companies know that they have a problem and that it is becoming your problem in that you have to keep removing messages.

What about performance impact?

Scanning all messages and removing potentially infected messages has a performance impact. During peak times, it is possible that scanning will cause significant delays in messaging performance. You need to consider the risk and the impact associated with scanning your messaging environment. There are some ways to reduce the impact:

- Scan mailbox and public folder stores during off-peak times to avoid impacting users.

- Scan only incoming messages and purchase client antivirus software that you can install on all of your client computers to scan outgoing messages.

- Offload all antivirus e-mail scanning to a standalone server that is dedicated to the purpose, and properly size it to handle the heavy loads during peak times.

Identifying and Closing Open Relays

A server configured for open relaying will accept Simple Mail Transfer Protocol (SMTP) messages from any SMTP domain and forward the message to any other SMTP domain. If your server is configured this way, an unauthorized user can send a single e-mail message with multiple recipients to your SMTP server and your server will forward the message to all the recipients. Users that send out Unsolicited Commercial E-mail (UCE), or spam, might use your server to send these e-mail messages.

If your server is configured for open relaying, you may experience performance problems, since your server could be sending thousands of emails. If your SMTP queue is growing rapidly or if you notice a significant increase in SMTP traffic, check your server for open relaying.

In addition, if your company has an open relay SMTP server, your company may also be put on a block list. Many companies use block lists to prevent connections from servers that are known for forwarding UCE. Companies may add your SMTP server to an internal list of open relay servers or they may subscribe to a block list that is maintained by a third-party company, such as Mail Abuse Prevention System (MAPS). (Block lists that are maintained by third-party companies are typically called Realtime Blackhole Lists or Relay Blocking Lists.) If your server does appear on the block list of a third-party company, companies that subscribe to the list will block all connections from your SMTP server.

Testing for open relays using Telnet

You can use Telnet to test whether your server is configured for open relaying. To test this, use a computer that is connected to the Internet and follow this procedure:

1. Open a command prompt and type **Telnet** *smtpservername* **25** (where *smtpservername* is the name of the specific SMTP server). The destination server will respond with a series of 250 commands.

2. Type ***Mail from:*** *user@domain.com* (where *user@domain.com* is a dummy account with a domain name different than your internal domain name).

   The server should respond with "250 2.1.0 user@domain.com Sender OK."

3. Type **Rcpt to:** *user2@domain2.com* (where *user2@domain2.com* is a dummy account with a domain name different than your internal domain name).

   If your server responds with "250 2.1.5 user2@domain2.com," it is configured for an open relaying. If your server responds with "550 5.7.1 Unable to relay for domain2.com," it is not relaying for that domain.

Closing open relays

Information on closing open relays in Exchange Server 2003 is located in Exchange Help. To locate the information, open Exchange System Manager, click **Help**, click **Help Topics**, and then click **Search**. Search for **Set Relay Restrictions** and then click the topic "**Set Relay Restrictions on Virtual Servers**."

Impact of Virus and Content Scanners on Messaging Functionality

One of the more difficult components to troubleshoot in messaging is third-party scanning software. Messages need to be scanned in order to stop virus infections and the propagation of virus infections to other e-mail systems on the Internet.

Over the past couple of years, companies have started to realize that their e-mail servers are being clogged with non-business related e-mail (e.g., personal e-mail between friends), Unsolicited Commercial E-mail (UCE; also known as spam), and even e-mail that is meant to maliciously harm the company.

Virus infections

Virus infections are bad news for a number of reasons:

- Lost productivity of end-users
- Poor server performance (the Melissa virus is a great example)
- Unable to process our important business messages
- Spreading the virus to other companies can cause a temporary e-mail block
- Publicity that impacts the stock value of a company

To prevent virus infections, antivirus software must be kept up to date. Antivirus software usually exists in several places in a company, including:

- *Firewalls or viruswalls*. Firewalls and viruswalls can be troublesome as many of them do not support all of the SMTP verbs available and may cause problems depending on the origination system and the type of message being sent.
- *E-mail servers*. Most antivirus software packages will scan the stores on a regular basis and will scan all new messages as they arrive.
- *File servers*. Users often pull attachments from file servers, so it is good to know that they will be virus free before they are sent.
- *Client computers*. In the event a virus gets past any of the other antivirus applications, you need to be aware that a client-side antivirus application may end up deleting messages through the Microsoft Outlook® client.

Content scanning

Content scanning is not just looking for virus infected files. Content scanning is utilized by many companies to:

- Combat spam.
- Keep users from sending proprietary information outside the company.
- Keep users from sending explicit e-mails to others.
- Keep outside e-mail that may lead to sexual harassment concerns from being sent to users.

The problem that occurs most often with content scanning is that many false positives can occur, leading to lost productivity and a great deal of administrative effort to fix the scanning solution.

Performance impact   While it is acknowledged that virus and content scanners are needed in many cases, the related performance decreases can be very significant. You might need to install extra CPUs and RAM to handle the load placed on your e-mail server by these scanners.

Administrative impact   Also, you need to be aware that positive scanner hits, as well as false positive hits, will mean that some messages are lost. Some users will assume something is wrong with the e-mail server when they do not get the e-mails that they are expecting, and this can lead to extra, unnecessary troubleshooting work since there is not a problem with your e-mail server. Be ready to check quarantine logs for messages as part of the troubleshooting process for lost messages.

Using the Telnet Command to Test the TCP Port Restrictions on a Firewall

If you feel that the firewall might be the source of a problem, you can use Telnet to test the firewall port restrictions. From inside the firewall to the Internet, you will need to find a server that will accept your session. For example, if you want to test whether SMTP is open and allowing traffic from inside the network to outside the network, you will need to have a target system somewhere outside the firewall that will accept SMTP commands. Basically, this is any e-mail server on the Internet. To test SMTP, use the following steps:

Test SMTP – Port 25

1. Click **Start**, click **Run**, type **CMD** and then click **OK**.

2. At the command prompt, type **telnet** *company.com* **25** (where *company.com* is the domain name of the e-mail server) and wait for the response.

   If the target is an Exchange Server 2003 server with a properly configured MX record and the firewall allows port 25 traffic outside the company, you will receive the following message:

   220 *company.com* (where *company.com* is the domain name of the e-mail server) Microsoft ESMTP MAIL Service, Version: 6.0.3790.0 ready at Sun, 10 Aug 2003 04:08:26 -0600

3. Type **quit** at the prompt to close the connection.

You can use this same procedure from outside the company to test the firewall and make sure port 25 is open to allow incoming e-mail traffic.

Test POP3 – Port 110 and 995

Generally, you will only allow remote network users to access Exchange Server 2003 using Post Office Protocol version 3 (POP3), since internal clients will be better served using the Outlook client. To test from outside the firewall, use the following steps:

1. Click **Start**, click **Run**, type **CMD** and then click **OK**.

2. At the command prompt, type **telnet** *company.com* **110** (where *company.com* is the domain name of the e-mail server) and wait for the response.

   If the target is an Exchange Server 2003 server and the firewall allows port 110 traffic from outside the company, you will receive the following message:

   +OK Microsoft Exchange Server 2003 POP3 server version 6.5.6944.0 *company.com* (where *company.com* is the domain name of the e-mail server) ready

3. Type **quit** at the prompt to close the connection.

4. Test 995, which is used for Secure Sockets Layer- (SSL) protected POP3 services, using the same process, but typing **995** instead of 110.

Test IMAP4 – Port 143 and 993

Generally, you will only allow remote network users to access Exchange Server 2003 using Internet Mail Access Protocol version 4rev1 (IMAP4), since internal clients will be better served using the Outlook client. To test from outside the firewall, use the following steps:

1. Click **Start**, click **Run**, type **CMD** and then click **OK**.

2. At the command prompt, type **telnet** *company.com* **143** (where *company.com* is the domain name of the e-mail server) and wait for the response.

   If the target is an Exchange 2003 server and the firewall allows port 143 traffic from outside the company, you will receive the following message:

   * OK Microsoft Exchange Server 2003 IMAP4rev1 server version 6.5.6944.0 *company.com* (where *company.com* is the domain name of the e-mail server) ready

3. Type **IMAP Logout** at the prompt to close the connection.

4. Test 993, which is used for SSL-protected IMAP4 services, using the same process, typing **993** instead of 143.

Other ports

You can use Telnet to test the firewall to see if other ports are open and verify that the server responds to the traffic type used by the port. For example, you can test Network News Transfer Protocol (NNTP) port availability to use port number 119. Once connected, you can send NNTP commands and verify that NNTP is functioning as expected.

Using Dcdiag and Netdiag to Verify the Network Infrastructure

The DCDiag command

DCDiag will perform the following:

- Verify that the domain can support Active Directory.

- Determine if it is possible to create an Active Directory forest.

- Determine if it is possible to add another domain controller to an existing domain.

- Determine if a Microsoft Windows 2000, Microsoft Windows XP, or Microsoft Windows Server™ 2003 computer can be added to the domain.

- Test replication between domain controllers.

- Report down servers.

- Test that all domain controllers are advertising their presence to other domain controllers.

DCDiag can be used to test the state of domain controllers in a forest. It will report any problems it finds.

/v   Verbose mode will provide more information in an easier-to-read format. The /v switch will also provide information about the Flexible Single Master Operation (FSMO) roles.

/f   The /f switch is used to point to a file for logging the results of the DCDiag command.

/?   The help switch will provide more information about the other options that are available for the DCDiag command.

The NetDiag command

NetDiag tests network connectivity by testing the following items:

- Network adapter interface information, including the:
  - Host name
  - IP address
  - Subnet mask
  - Default gateway
  - DNS server
  - Windows Internet Name Service (WINS) server
- Domain membership
- Loopback ping test
- Default gateway ping test
- Network basic input/output system (NetBIOS) name check
- Winsock test
- DNS test

- Domain controller discovery test
- Trust relationship test
- Lightweight Directory Access Protocol (LDAP) test
- Internet Protocol Security (IPSec) test

/v   The tests performed by NetDiag will alert you to many possible problems. You
        can expand on the result messages by using the /v switch to turn on verbose
        mode.

/f   The tests performed by NetDiag can result in a large amount of output. It may be
        necessary to send the resulting information to others to review. Using the /l
        switch will capture the information to a log file in the same directory as the
        netdiag.exe file.

/?   The help switch will provide more information about the other options that are
        available for the NetDiag command.

Using Service Logs

By default, services that log activity store their logs in the *systemroot*\system32\logfiles folder.

The Web, SMTP, and NNTP logs are especially relevant to Exchange troubleshooting. For example, if your server is unable to transmit messages to a remote server across the Internet, you may wish to enable SMTP logging so that you can review the SMTP activity between the two servers.

The DNS log is located in the *systemroot*\system32\dns folder. The DNS log file maintains DNS error messages.

Moving Logs

Most of the log files can be moved by making changes in the properties of the service. For example, in **Exchange System Manager**, you can expand the **Server** and the **Protocols** nodes, and then expand the **SMTP** node. Right-click **Default SMTP Virtual Server** and click **Properties**.

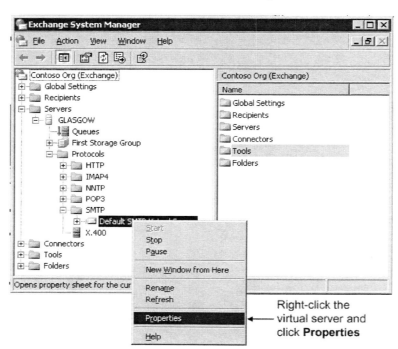

Right-click the virtual server and click **Properties**

Select the check box to **Enable logging**, and click **Properties** to make changes as needed.

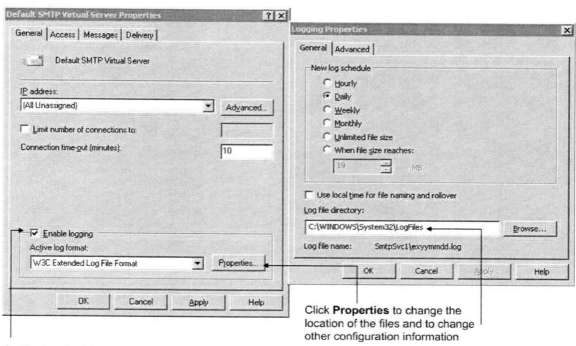

Enable the check box to
enable logging for the service

Click **Properties** to change the
location of the files and to change
other configuration information

Unit 8: Troubleshooting Security Issues

Impact of Virus and Content Scanners on Messaging Functionality

One of the more difficult components to troubleshoot in messaging is third-party scanning software. Messages need to be scanned to stop virus infections and the propagation of virus infections to other e-mail systems on the Internet.

Over the past couple of years, companies have started to realize that their e-mail servers are being clogged with non-business related e-mail (e.g., personal e-mail between friends), Unsolicited Commercial E-mail (UCE; also known as spam), and even e-mail that is meant to maliciously harm the company.

Virus infections

Virus infections are bad news for a number of reasons:

- Lost productivity of end-users
- Poor server performance (the Melissa virus is a great example)
- Unable to process important business messages
- Spreading the virus to other companies can cause a temporary e-mail block
- Publicity that impacts the stock value of a company

To prevent virus infections, antivirus software must be kept up to date. Antivirus software usually exists in several places in a company, including:

- *Firewalls or viruswalls.* Firewalls and viruswalls can be troublesome as many of them do not support all of the SMTP verbs available and may cause problems depending on the origination system and the type of message being sent.
- *E-mail servers.* Most antivirus software packages will scan the stores on a regular basis and will scan all new messages as they arrive.
- *File servers.* Users often pull attachments from file servers, so it is good to know that they will be virus free before they are sent.
- *Client computers.* In the event a virus gets past any of the other antivirus applications, you need to be aware that a client-side antivirus application may end up deleting messages through the Microsoft® Outlook® client.

Content scanning

Content scanning is not just looking for virus infected files. Content scanning is utilized by many companies to:

- Combat spam.
- Keep users from sending proprietary information outside the company.
- Keep users from sending explicit e-mails to others.
- Keep outside e-mail that may lead to sexual harassment concerns from being sent to users.

The problem that occurs most often with content scanning is that many false positives can occur, leading to lost productivity and a great deal of administrative effort to fix the scanning solution.

Performance impact

While it is acknowledged that virus and content scanners are needed in many cases, the related performance decreases can be very significant. You might need to install extra CPUs and RAM to handle the load placed on your e-mail server by these scanners.

Administrative impact

Also, you need to be aware that positive scanner hits, as well as false positive hits, will mean that some messages are lost. Some users will assume something is wrong with the e-mail server when they do not get the e-mails that they are expecting, and this can lead to extra, unnecessary troubleshooting work since there is not a problem with your e-mail server. Be ready to check quarantine logs for messages as part of the troubleshooting process for lost messages.

Implementing and Testing RPC over HTTP

Installing RPC over HTTP Proxy service

The first step to enabling remote procedure call (RPC) over HTTP is to install the RPC over HTTP Proxy component to Microsoft Windows Server™ 2003. You must install this component on all Microsoft Exchange® Server 2003 front-end servers and on the back-end server if you are not using a front-end server. To install this component, follow these steps:

1. On the Exchange Server 2003 server running Windows Server 2003, in Add or Remove Programs, click **Add/Remove Windows Components**.

2. In the Windows Components Wizard, on the **Windows Components** page, click **Networking Services** and then click **Details**.

3. In Networking Services, select the **RPC over HTTP Proxy** check box and then click **OK**.

4. On the **Windows Components** page, click **Next** to install the RPC over HTTP Proxy component.

Configuring the RPC virtual directory

After you configure your Exchange front-end server to use RPC over HTTP, you must configure the RPC virtual directory in Internet Information Services (IIS). To configure the RPC virtual directory, follow these steps:

1. Start Internet Information Services Manager.

2. In Internet Information Services Manager, in the console tree, expand the server you want, expand Web Sites, expand Default Web Site, right-click the RPC virtual directory, and then click **Properties**.

3. In RPC Properties, on the **Directory Security** tab, in Authentication and access control, click **Edit**.

4. Under Authenticated access, select the **Basic authentication (password is sent in clear text)** check box and then click **OK**.

5. To save your settings, click **Apply** and then click **OK**.

Configuring RPC over HTTP port numbers

After configuring the RPC virtual directory, you must configure the Exchange servers and the global catalog server to use specific port numbers. To configure the RPC Proxy server to use specified port numbers for RPC over HTTP, follow these steps:

1. Log on to the RPC proxy server. Click **Start**, click **Run**, type **regedit** and then click **OK**.

2. In Registry Editor, in the console tree, browse to *HKEY_LOCAL_MACHINE*\Software\Microsoft\Rpc\RpcProxy and then click **RpcProxy**.

3. In the details pane, right-click **ValidPorts** and then click **Modify**.

4. In the **Edit String** dialog box, in the **Value data** box, type the following and then click **OK**:

*ExchangeServer:***593;***ExchangeServerFQDN:***593;
*ExchangeServer:***6001-6002;***ExchangeServerFQDN:***6001-6002;
*ExchangeServer:***6004;***ExchangeServerFQDN:***6004;
*GlobalCatalogServer:***593;***GlobalCatalogServerFQDN:***593;
*GlobalCatalogServer:***6004;***GlobalCatalogServerFQDN:***6004

The variables *ExchangeServer* and *GlobalCatalogServer* are the network basic input/output system (NetBIOS) names of your Exchange server and global catalog server. *ExchangeFQDN* and *GlobalCatalogServerFQDN* are the fully qualified domain names of your Exchange server and global catalog server. In the registry key, continue to list all servers in the corporate network with which the RPC Proxy server will need to communicate.

Configuring global catalog servers to use specified port numbers

To configure the global catalog servers to use specified port numbers for RPC over HTTP, follow these steps:

1. In Registry Editor, browse to *HKEY_LOCAL_MACHINE*\SYSTEM\CurrentControlSet\Services\NTDS\Parameters and then click **Parameters**.

2. From the **Edit** menu, point to **New** and then click **Multi-String value**.

3. In the details pane, type **NSPI interface protocol sequences** and then press **Enter**.

4. Right-click the **NSPI interface protocol sequences** multi-string value, and then click **Modify**.

5. In the **Edit Multi-String** dialog box, in the **Value data** box, type **ncacn_http:6004** and then click **OK**.

6. Close Registry Editor and restart the server.

Creating an Outlook profile to use with RPC over HTTP

Before you can configure an Outlook profile to use RPC over HTTP, you must install the Microsoft Windows® XP patch Q331320. To create an Outlook profile to use RPC over HTTP on a computer that already has a MAPI profile for your user account, follow these steps:

1. On the **Start** menu, right-click **E-mail Microsoft Office Outlook** and then click **Properties**.

2. In Mail Setup, under Profiles, click **Show Profiles**.

3. In Mail, click **Add**.

4. In New Profile, in the **Profile Name** box, type **RPC-HTTP** and then click **OK**.

5. In the E-mail Accounts Wizard, verify that the **Add a new e-mail account** check box is selected and then click **Next**.

6. On the **Server Type** page, click **Microsoft Exchange Server** and then click **Next**.

7. On the **Exchange Server Settings** page, perform the following steps:
   - In the **Microsoft Exchange Server** box, type the Exchange server name.
   - Verify that the **Use Cached Exchange Mode** check box is selected.
   - In the **User Name** box, type your username.

8. Click **More Settings**. In the **Microsoft Exchange Server** dialog box, click **Connection**.

9. On the **Connection** tab, select the **Connect to my Exchange mailbox using HTTP** check box and then click **Exchange Proxy Settings**.

10. On the **Exchange Proxy Settings** page, perform the following steps and then click **OK**:

    - In the **Use this URL to connect to my proxy server for Exchange** box, type *ExchangeserverFQDN* (where *ExchangeFQDN* is the fully qualified domain name of your Exchange server).

    - Verify that the **Connect using SSL only** check box is selected.

    - Select the **Mutually authenticate the session when connecting with SSL** check box.

    - In the **Principle name for proxy server** box, type **msstd:**RPCProxyServerFQDN

    - Select the **On fast networks, connect to Exchange using HTTP first, then connect using TCP/IP** check box.

11. In the Proxy authentication settings area, in the **Use this authentication when connecting to my proxy server for Exchange** box, click **Basic Authentication**.

12. In the **Microsoft Exchange Server** dialog box, click **OK**.

13. In the E-mail Accounts Wizard, click **Next** and then click **Finish**.

14. In the **Mail** dialog box, verify the **Prompt for a profile to be used** check box is selected and then click **OK**.

Verifying that Outlook is communicating with Exchange by using RPC over HTTP

To verify that Outlook is connecting to the Exchange Server using RPC over HTTP, follow these steps:

1. Open Outlook using a profile that is configured to use RPC over HTTP.

2. From your desktop, in the **Application tray**, in the bottom right corner, hold down the **CTRL** key, right-click the **Outlook** icon, and then click **Connection Status**.

3. In Connection Status, verify that the connection type is HTTP.

Implementing SSL for Exchange Server 2003

One of the options for enabling secure email in an Exchange Server 2003 organization is to implement Secure Sockets Layer (SSL) on the protocol virtual servers used for Internet clients. By configuring SSL, you can ensure that all e-mail related traffic, including users' credentials, is encrypted. In order to implement SSL, you must perform three separate steps.

Install a Web Server certificate on the Exchange server

A Web Server certificate includes the Server Authentication application policy required for SSL encryption. You can use a single Web Server certificate for all SSL-enabled protocols on the Exchange server.

To request and install a certificate for the default Web site on a server, use the following procedure:

1. Open Internet Information Services (IIS) Manager from the Administrative Tools folder.

2. In Internet Information Services Manager, in the console tree, expand *servername* (where *servername* is the name of the local computer) and then expand Web Sites.

3. In the console tree, right-click **Default Web Site** and then click **Properties**.

4. In the **Default Web Site Properties** dialog box, click **Directory Security**.

5. On the **Directory Security** tab, click **Server Certificate**.

6. In the Welcome to the Web Server Certificate Wizard, on the **Welcome** page, click **Next**.

7. On the **Server Certificate** page, verify that the **Create a new certificate** check box is selected and then click **Next**.

8. On the **Delayed or Immediate Request** page, choose how to send the request to the certification authority (CA). If you are using a CA that is accessible online in your organization, click **Send the request immediately to an online certification authority** and then click **Next**. If you are creating a certificate request to send to an offline commercial CA, select the **Prepare the request now, but send it later** check box. When you complete the wizard, the server will generate a key that you can then send to an offline CA. (If you choose to send the request to an offline CA, you will need to restart the wizard to install the certificate when you receive it.)

9. On the **Name and Security Settings** page, in the **Name** box, type a name for the certificate and then click **Next**.

10. On the **Organization Information** page, in the **Organization** box, type *organizationname* in the **Organizational Unit** box, type *OUName* and then click **Next**.

11. On the **Your Site's Common Name** page, in the **Common name** box, type *serverFQDN* (where *serverFQDN* is the name that clients will use to connect to the server) and then click **Next**.

12. On the **Geographical Information** page, in the **State/province** box, and in the **City/locality** box, type the required information and click **Next**.

13. On the **SSL Port** page, in the **SSL port this web site should use** box, verify that 443 is specified and then click **Next**.

14. On the **Choose a Certification Authority** page, in the **Certification Authorities** box, verify that the correct CA is selected and then click **Next**.

15. On the **Certificate Request Submission** page, click **Next** to submit the request and then click **Finish** to complete the wizard. The certificate is now installed if the chosen CA is online and configured to automatically approve certificate requests.

Configure Exchange virtual servers to use SSL

Once you have obtained and installed the Web Server certificate, you need to configure each of the required protocol virtual servers to require SSL. You can use the same certificate for all the protocol virtual servers, but you must configure each protocol virtual server separately.

To configure the HTTP virtual server to use the certificate to secure the default Web site that is using SSL, use the following procedure:

1. Open Internet Information Services Manager from the Administrative Tools folder.

2. In Internet Information Services Manager, in the console tree, expand *servername* (where *servername* is the name of the local computer) and then expand Web Sites.

3. In the console tree, right-click **Default Web Site** and then click **Properties**.

4. In the **Default Web Site Properties** dialog box, on the **Directory Security** tab, in the Secure communications area, click **Edit**.

5. In the **Secure Communications** dialog box, select the **Require secure channel (SSL)** check box, select the **Require 128-bit encryption** check box, and then click **OK**.

6. On the **Directory Security** tab, in the Authentication and access control area, click **Edit**.

7. In the **Authentication Methods** dialog box, select the **Basic authentication (password is sent in clear text)** check box and then click **Yes** to acknowledge the warning.

8. Clear the **Integrated Windows Authentication** and **Enable Anonymous Access** check boxes, and then click **OK**.

9. In the Default Web site **Properties** dialog box, click **OK**.

10. In all **Inheritance Overrides** dialog boxes, click **OK**. Close Internet Information Services (IIS) Manager.

To use the certificate to secure the default IMAP virtual server, use the following procedure:

1. Open Exchange System Manager and locate the server. Expand the server object, expand the Protocols container, and expand the IMAP4 container.

2. Right-click **Default IMAP4 Virtual Server** and click **Properties**.

3. On the **Access** tab, click **Certificates**.

4. In the Welcome to the Web Server Certificate Wizard, on the **Welcome** page, click **Next**.

5. On the **Server Certificate** page, verify that the **Assign an existing certificate** check box is selected and then click **Next**.

6. On the **Available Certificates** page, click the server authentication certificate for the web server. Click **Next**.

7. Click **Next** and then click **Finish**.

8. The previous steps assigned the Web Server certificate to the IMAP4 virtual server. To configure the virtual server to accept only SSL connections, on the **Access** tab, click **Communication** and then select the **Require secure channel** check box and the **Require 128 bit encryption** check box.

9. Click **OK** to close the **Security** page, and then click **OK** to close the **IMAP4 Virtual Server Properties** page.

Configure e-mail applications for SSL

After you configure the protocol virtual servers to require SSL, you must also configure all e-mail clients to connect to the Exchange server by using the SSL-enabled port instead of the default port. After SSL is enabled on a virtual server, the virtual server will not accept connections to the default port.

To configure Microsoft Outlook Express to use SSL for an IMAP account, use the following procedure:

1. Open Outlook Express. Click **Tools** and then click **Accounts**.

2. Click the account that you want to modify and then click **Properties**.

3. On the **Advanced** tab, select the **This server requires a secure connection (SSL)** check box under Server Port numbers. If the server requires SSL for both IMAP and SMTP, select the secure connection option for both IMAP and SMTP.

Using S/MIME to Sign and Seal E-Mail Messages

One option for securing e-mail is to send e-mail messages using S/MIME. If you have S/MIME configured, you can digitally sign and encrypt e-mail messages. To configure an e-mail client to support S/MIME, you must first obtain and install a digital certificate on the computer where you are running the e-mail client. Then you must obtain a digital signature for each user with whom you want to exchange secure email. The procedure used to obtain and install the digital certificate varies between different clients.

Requesting a certificate from an online CA

To obtain a digital certificate using an online Certificate Authority, use the following procedure (this procedure illustrates how to obtain a certificate from a Windows Server 2003 Enterprise CA):

1. Connect to the CA Web site at https:*servername*/certsrv. Log on using your domain username and password.

2. On the initial screen, click **Request a Certificate** and then click **Next**.

3. On the **Request a Certificate** screen, click **User Certificate** and then click **Next**.

4. On the **User Certificate, Identifying Information** screen, click **Submit**.

5. Click **Yes**, click **Install this Certificate**, then click **Yes** and close your browser window.

Configuring Outlook 2003 for S/MIME

After installing all digital certificates, you can configure Microsoft Outlook 2003 to use the certificates to enable digital signature and encryption capabilities. To configure Outlook to use the certificates, use the following procedure:

1. Open Outlook. On the **Tools** menu, click **Options**.

2. In the **Options** dialog box, click the **Security** tab, and then in the **Encrypted** box, click **Settings**.

3. In the **Security Settings Preferences** dialog box, in the **Security Settings Name** box, type a logical name for the e-mail digital certificate.

4. In the **Certificates and Algorithms** box, in the **Signing Certificate** box, select a signing certificate, and then in the **Hash Algorithm** box, select an algorithm.

5. In the **Certificates and Algorithms** box, in the **Encryption Certificate** box, select an encryption certificate, and then in the **Encryption Algorithm** box, select an algorithm.

6. Click **OK** to close the **Change Security Settings** dialog box.

7. To configure the same security settings for all e-mails you send, on the **Security** tab, in the **Encrypted** box, select or clear the following check boxes based on your business needs:

   • **Encrypt contents and attachments for outgoing messages**

   • **Add digital signature to outgoing messages**

   • **Send clear text signed message when sending signed messages**

   • **Request S/MIME receipt for all S/MIME signed messages**

8. Click **OK** to close the **Options** dialog box.

Configuring Outlook Express for S/MIME

After installing all digital certificates, you can configure Outlook Express to use the certificates to enable digital signature and encryption capabilities. To configure Outlook Express to use the certificates, use the following procedure:

1. Open Outlook Express. On the **Tools** menu, click **Accounts**.

2. Click the account that you are configuring and then click **Properties**.

3. In the **Signing Certificate** box, click **Select**, select a signing certificate, and then click **OK**.

4. In the **Encryption Certificate** box, click **Select**, select a signing certificate, and then click **OK**.

5. Click **OK**.

Using the Telnet Command to Test the TCP Port Restrictions on a Firewall

If you feel that the firewall might be the source of a problem, you can use Telnet to test the firewall port restrictions. From inside the firewall to the Internet, you will need to find a server that will accept your session. For example, if you want to test whether SMTP is open and allowing traffic from inside the network to outside the network, you will need to have a target system somewhere outside the firewall that will accept SMTP commands. Basically, this is any e-mail server on the Internet. To test SMTP, use the following steps:

Test SMTP – Port 25

1. Click **Start**, click **Run**, type **CMD** and then click **OK**.

2. At the command prompt, type **telnet** *company.com* **25** (where *company.com* is the domain name of the e-mail server) and wait for the response.

   If the target is an Exchange Server 2003 server with a properly configured MX record and the firewall allows port 25 traffic outside the company, you will receive the following message:

   220 *company.com* (where *company.com* is the domain name of the e-mail server) Microsoft ESMTP MAIL Service, Version: 6.0.3790.0 ready at Sun, 10 Aug 2003 04:08:26 -0600

3. Type **quit** at the prompt to close the connection.

You can use this same procedure from outside the company to test the firewall and make sure port 25 is open to allow incoming e-mail traffic.

Test POP3 – Port 110 and 995

Generally, you will only allow remote network users to access Exchange Server 2003 using Post Office Protocol version 3 (POP3), since internal clients will be better served using the Outlook client. To test from outside the firewall, use the following steps:

1. Click **Start**, click **Run**, type **CMD** and then click **OK**.

2. At the command prompt, type **telnet** *company.com* **110** (where *company.com* is the domain name of the e-mail server) and wait for the response.

   If the target is an Exchange Server 2003 server and the firewall allows port 110 traffic from outside the company, you will receive the following message:

   +OK Microsoft Exchange Server 2003 POP3 server version 6.5.6944.0 *company.com* (where *company.com* is the domain name of the e-mail server) ready

3. Type **quit** at the prompt to close the connection.

4. Test 995, which is used for SSL-protected POP3 services, using the same process, but typing **995** instead of 110.

Test IMAP4 – Port 143 and 993

Generally, you will only allow remote network users to access Exchange Server 2003 using Internet Message Access Protocol version 4rev1 (IMAP4), since internal clients will be better served using the Outlook client. To test from outside the firewall, use the following steps:

1. Click **Start**, click **Run**, type **CMD** and then click **OK**.

2. At the command prompt, type **telnet** *company.com* **143** (where *company.com* is the domain name of the e-mail server) and wait for the response.

   If the target is an Exchange 2003 server and the firewall allows port 143 traffic from outside the company, you will receive the following message:

   * OK Microsoft Exchange Server 2003 IMAP4rev1 server version 6.5.6944.0 *company.com* (where *company.com* is the domain name of the e-mail server) ready

3. Type **IMAP Logout** at the prompt to close the connection.

4. Test 993, which is used for SSL-protected IMAP4 services, using the same process, typing **993** instead of 143.

Other ports

You can use Telnet to test the firewall to see if other ports are open and verify that the server responds to the traffic type used by the port. For example, you can test Network News Transfer Protocol (NNTP) port availability to use port number 119. Once connected, you can send NNTP commands and verify that NNTP is functioning as expected.

Using DcDiag and NetDiag to Verify the Network Infrastructure

The DCDiag command   DCDiag will perform the following:

- Verify that the domain can support Microsoft Active Directory®.
- Determine if it is possible to create an Active Directory forest.
- Determine if it is possible to add another domain controller to an existing domain.
- Determine if a Microsoft Windows 2000, Windows XP, or Windows Server 2003 computer can be added to the domain.
- Test replication between domain controllers.
- Report down servers.
- Test that all domain controllers are advertising their presence to other domain controllers.

DCDiag can be used to test the state of domain controllers in a forest. It will report any problems it finds.

/v   Verbose mode will provide more information in an easier to read format. The /v switch will also provide information about the Flexible Single Master Operation (FSMO) roles.

/f   The /f switch is used to point to a file for logging the results of the DCDiag command.

/?   The help switch will provide more information about the other options that are available for the DCDiag command.

The NetDiag command   NetDiag tests network connectivity by testing the following items:

- Network adapter interface information, including the:
  - Host name
  - IP address
  - Subnet mask
  - Default gateway
  - DNS server
  - Windows Internet Name Service (WINS) server
- Domain membership
- Loopback ping test
- Default gateway ping test
- NetBIOS name check
- Winsock test
- DNS test
- Domain controller discovery test
- Trust relationship test
- Lightweight Directory Access Protocol (LDAP) test
- Internet Protocol Security (IPSec) test

/v   The tests performed by NetDiag will alert you to many possible problems. You can expand on the result messages by using the /v switch to turn on verbose mode.

/l   The tests performed by NetDiag can result in a large amount of output. It may also be necessary to send the resulting information to others to review. Using the /l switch will capture the information to a log file in the same directory as the netdiag.exe file.

/?   The help switch will provide more information about the other options that are available for the NetDiag command.

Verifying That a Server Is Online

During troubleshooting, you may need to verify remotely that a server is online. This verification can include several steps. In most cases, you should start by verifying basic network connectivity, then verify name resolution, and then verify service availability.

1. To verify network connectivity, ping the IP address of the remote server. If the ping is successful, move on to the next step in troubleshooting. If the ping is not successful, determine whether there is a network failure by pinging another server in the same subnet, or by using **pathping** or **tracert** to determine where the failure occurs.

2. If the ping is successful, ping the fully qualified domain name of the server. If the ping is successful, move on to the next step. If the ping is not successful, use tools such as NSLookup or DNSLint to determine the DNS zone information and server configuration. You may also need to check the Hosts file; in most cases, the Hosts file should not contain any information.

3. In some cases, clients may need to connect to the server using NetBIOS names. This is true if you have older clients such as Microsoft Windows 95, Microsoft Windows 98, or Microsoft Windows NT® workstations on your network. To verify NetBIOS connectivity, use the **Net Use** command, or use Netdiag.exe. You can also use the **Browstat.exe** command (included in the Windows Server 2003 Support Tools) to perform detailed NetBIOS browser troubleshooting.

4. If you can successfully connect to the server using host and NetBIOS names, the next step in troubleshooting is to test protocol connectivity. The best tool to test e-mail-related protocol connectivity is Telnet. If you cannot connect to the server using Telnet, verify that the required protocol is not blocked by a network device.

5. If you cannot connect to the server using Telnet, confirm that the required services are running on the Exchange server. The services that must be running on a front-end server are discussed in Securing a Front-End and Back-End Server Infrastructure in this Toolkit resource.

   The following services must be running on a back-end server:

   • Exchange System Attendant

   • Exchange store

   • Exchange System Manager

   • Windows Management Instrumentation

   • Microsoft Exchange Routing Engine

   • IIS Admin Service

   • SMTP

   • World Wide Web Publishing Service

   • Additional services, like NNTP, Exchange IMAP4, Exchange POP3, HTTP SSL Microsoft Exchange Event Service, Microsoft Exchange Site Replication Service, and Microsoft Exchange MTA Stacks, may be required to support Internet protocol clients or for compatibility with previous versions of Exchange.

Note These services are dependent on Windows Server 2003 services. View the properties of each service to confirm the service dependencies.

To verify the status of the services on a remote computer, you can connect to the computer using a custom Computer Management Microsoft Management Console (MMC) or use Remote Desktop. If the required services are functional on the server, verify that the Exchange mailbox and public folder stores are mounted. You can use the Exchange System Manager to verify the mounted stores.

Unit 9: Troubleshooting the Migration to Exchange 2003

Routing Messages During Migration

In most large organizations, the migration from Microsoft® Exchange Server 5.5 to Microsoft Exchange Server 2003 will take an extended period of time. Because of this, you need to plan for an extended period of coexistence, during which you will need to support both Exchange versions. The coexistence is fairly easy to manage if you are performing a standard migration, upgrading an existing Exchange 5.5 organization to Exchange 2003. However, if you are performing an external migration from an Exchange 5.5 organization to a new Exchange 2003 organization, coexistence can be quite complicated. One of the complicating factors is determining the best way to route messages between the two organizations.

The migration of the Contoso Exchange 5.5 organization to the Northwind Traders Exchange 2003 organization is one example of an external migration.

The following diagram illustrates the two networks before migration.

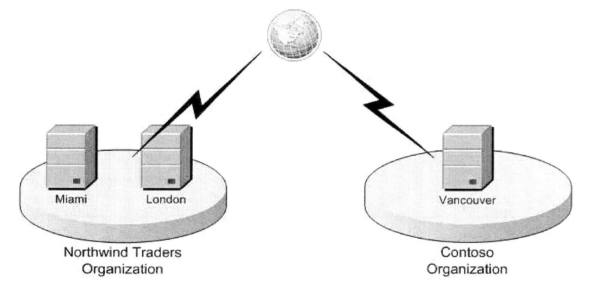

Northwind Traders
Organization

Contoso
Organization

Routing Internet Messages

In most migration scenarios, both Exchange organizations will already be configured to support inbound and outbound Internet e-mail. In the Exchange 5.5 organization, an Internet Mail Service connector is used to route messages to the Internet. In the Exchange 2003 organization, a Simple Mail Transfer Protocol (SMTP) connector serves the same purpose. For both organizations, mail exchanger (MX) records on the Internet DNS servers point to the appropriate SMTP servers for inbound messages.

There are several coexistence strategies that can be used during the migration:

1. *Maintaining the existing connectors and unique e-mail addresses.* If each organization is maintaining a different SMTP address during the migration, you do not have to make any changes to the existing configuration. For example, in a typical scenario, all of the users at Contoso have an SMTP address of alias@contoso.msft and all the users at Northwind Traders have an SMTP address of alias@nwtraders.msft. As the mailboxes are moved from Contoso to Northwind Traders, you can configure the new mailboxes with just nwtraders.msft addresses, and then the Internet routing configuration does not need to change.

2. *Removing one of the existing connectors and maintaining unique e-mail addresses.* If you want to remove one of the Internet connections, you can change the routing configuration so that all inbound SMTP e-mail is sent to one of the organizations and then routed to the other organization. For example, you may want to retain only the SMTP connector at Northwind Traders. To enable this, modify the MX records for Contoso.com on the Internet DNS servers to point to the SMTP bridgehead server at Northwind Traders. Then configure message routing between the two organizations.

3. *Using the same SMTP address in both organizations.* Frequently, companies must maintain the same SMTP addresses for users during and after the migration, since the source SMTP address is known outside the organization. In some cases, the destination organization and the source organization may have the same SMTP address. In other cases, the destination organization may have a different SMTP address but users must be able use both addresses. To enable this, configure the destination organization to accept Internet e-mail sent to both SMTP domains and then configure message routing between the two organizations.

Routing messages between organizations

In addition to Internet e-mail, you will also need to maintain message routing between the two organizations during the migration. You have two options when configuring the message routing:

1. *Organizations with different SMTP addresses.* The easiest way to enable message routing between the organizations is to configure SMTP routing between the two organizations. If both organizations are maintaining their Internet mail connections during the migration, use the existing connections. If you are removing one of the Internet connections, implement an internal SMTP routing solution. For example, if you are removing the Internet connection at Contoso, you could configure an SMTP connector from the Northwind Traders organization to the Exchange 5.5 organization using an address space of Contoso.com and a smart host in the Contoso organization. Then configure the Internet Mail Service at Contoso to forward all e-mail to a smart host in the Northwind Traders organization for all outgoing Internet messages.

2. *Organizations with the same SMTP address.* If both organizations are using the same SMTP address, use an SMTP connector to route messages between the two organizations by configuring the two organizations to share the same SMTP address space. As an alternative, if the two organizations have unique X.400 addresses, configure an X.400 connector between the two organizations. If you do configure an X.400 connector, you must ensure that the X.400 address for each mailbox is accurate.

To learn how to configure an X.400 connector in Exchange 2003, open Exchange System Manager Online Help and locate the article entitled "Configuring Message Routing." Review the topics that deal with configuring an X.400 transport stack and connector. To learn how to configure an X.400 connector in Exchange 5.5, open Exchange Administrator Online Help and locate the topic entitled "X.400 connector."

Troubleshooting Addressing Errors

Another complicating factor when performing an external migration from an Exchange 5.5 organization to a new Exchange 2003 organization is maintaining accurate addressing information in both organizations to ensure that users can send information between the two companies, as well as maintain Internet e-mail functionality.

Organization addressing issues

When you perform the migration from an Exchange 5.5 organization to a new Exchange Server organization, you must deal with several addressing issues at the organization level:

- *Managing migrated mailbox addresses.* When a mailbox is moved from an Exchange 5.5 organization to an Exchange 2003 organization using a tool like the Exchange Server Migration Wizard, the mailbox is not deleted from the Exchange 5.5 server. If you have a connection agreement configured to replicate information from Microsoft Active Directory® to the Exchange 5.5 organization, a custom recipient is created in Exchange 5.5 organization for the migrated mailbox. This indicates that the Exchange 5.5 organization contains a mailbox and a custom recipient with the same name as in the Exchange 2003 organization, and the users with mailboxes on the Exchange 5.5 servers will have to choose which recipient to use when sending e-mail. To resolve this, delete the mailboxes from the Exchange 5.5 servers when you migrate the mailboxes to Exchange Server 2003.

- *Using the same SMTP domain name.* In many cases, users must retain the same SMTP e-mail address after a migration. In some cases, you may be using the same SMTP address in both organizations. In other cases, a user may need to continue to use the old Exchange 5.5 SMTP address for a period of time after the migration. When a mailbox is moved to the Exchange 2003 organization, the mailbox is assigned the SMTP address for the new organization, but it also retains the SMTP and X.400 address that it had in the Exchange 5.5 organization. If you need to modify mailbox addresses, you can create a recipient policy or assign SMTP addresses to individual mailboxes.

- *Managing distribution lists or mail-enabled group memberships.* When you configure a connection agreement to replicate information from Exchange 5.5 to Active Directory, any distribution lists are migrated as contact items with e-mail addresses pointing to the distribution lists in the Exchange 5.5 organization. Any mail sent to one of these contact items from the Exchange 2003 organization is routed to the Exchange 5.5 server, which expands the membership list and delivers the messages to mailboxes. Before migration, distribution lists on the Exchange 5.5 server contained only mailboxes on the Exchange 5.5 organization. Since some of those mailboxes have been moved to the Exchange 2003 server, you must update the distribution lists to make sure that the address lists now point to the correct mailboxes. Also, as you migrate more of the mailboxes, you will also need to implement mail-enabled groups in the Exchange 2003 organization. These groups may contain both Exchange 2003 mailboxes and contact items for Exchange 5.5 mailboxes. The only way to avoid errors in message delivery to distribution lists or mail-enabled groups during migration is to modify the membership lists as the mailboxes are migrated.

- *Address book views cannot be migrated.* If address book views have been used in Exchange 5.5, create address lists in Exchange 2003 to provide the same functionality.

Client address issues   In some cases, addressing issues derive from client configuration issues, including the following:

- *Using the personal address book.* If a client is configured to use the personal address book (PAB) rather than the global address list (GAL) when resolving e-mail addresses, messages may not be delivered to the correct mailbox. For example, a user may have stored the address for a mailbox on the Exchange 5.5 server in the PAB. When that mailbox is migrated to the Exchange 2003 server, the GAL will be updated. However, if the client is configured to resolve e-mail addresses using the PAB, any message the user sends to the mailbox will still be routed to the Exchange 5.5 server. You can correct this error by reconfiguring the client to resolve e-mail addresses using the GAL, or the client can update the PAB information.

- *Replying to messages with the old e-mail address.* Users may experience errors when replying to old e-mail messages during a migration. This can happen when a user sends a message from their Exchange 5.5 e-mail account and then the mailbox is moved to the Exchange 2003 server. When other users reply to the message, the reply address is still configured as the Exchange 5.5 mailbox; as a result, the message will not be delivered to the correct mailbox. The only way to address this error is to educate users to re-enter the name of the recipient when they reply to e-mail messages. By re-entering the name, the correct mailbox will be selected from the GAL.

Verifying That the SIDHistory Attribute Is Populated on Migrated Objects

One option that is available when migrating users' accounts from one domain to another is to populate the **SIDHistory** attribute in the new user accounts. If you choose this option, the attribute is populated with the user or group Security IDs (SIDs) from the source domain. The can be used to provide access to resources in the source domain after the user accounts have been migrated to the destination domain.

Using ADSIEdit to view the SIDHistory attribute

You can use adsiedit.msc to view the **SIDHistory** attribute for a user or group account.

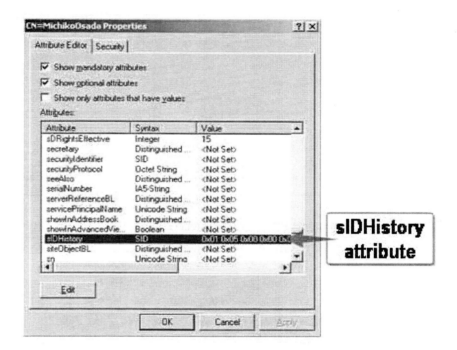

To view the **SIDHistory** attribute of a user or group account, following these steps:

1. Open a **Run** command and type **adsiedit.msc**

2. Expand the domain container and browse to the container that contains the user or group account.

3. Right-click the user or group name and click **Properties**. Browse to the **SIDHistory** attribute. If the value of the attribute is not set, **SIDHistory** was not migrated with the user account.

Configuring a Shared SMTP Address Space

As a company migrates from an Exchange 5.5 organization to a different Exchange Server 2003 organization, the company may need to share a common SMTP address space.

Exchange Server 2003 treats e-mail messages differently depending on whether Exchange Server 2003 is authoritative or non-authoritative for a particular SMTP address space. To determine if Exchange 2003 is authoritative or non-authoritative for an SMTP address space, perform the following steps:

1. Start **Exchange System Manager**, expand **Recipients**, and then click **Recipient Policies**.

2. In the **Recipient Policies** pane, right-click a recipient policy, and then click **Properties**.

3. On **the E-Mail Addresses (Policy)** tab, click **SMTP**, and then click **Edit**.

4. Examine the setting for the **This Exchange Organization is responsible for all mail delivery to this address** check box. If the check box is selected, Exchange Server 2003 is authoritative for the SMTP domain. If the check box is not selected, Exchange Server 2003 is non-authoritative for the SMTP domain.

If Exchange Server 2003 is configured as authoritative for an SMTP address space, it will accept inbound messages for the domain and attempt delivery of the message to a recipient in the organization. If the recipient does not exist in the organization, a non-delivery report (NDR) is created. If Exchange Server 2003 is not authoritative for the SMTP address space, but the SMTP connector to the Internet is configured to route for that SMTP address space, the server will accept inbound messages for the address space and attempt delivery of the message within the organization. If the recipient cannot be located, the Exchange server will attempt to route the message to another organization by using DNS or an SMTP connector with the required address space.

The following procedure describes how to configure a shared SMTP address space between two Exchange organizations. This procedure assumes that the Exchange Server 2003 organization is not authoritative for the SMTP address space but that Internet messages sent to the SMTP address space are routed through the Exchange Server 2003 organization. This procedure also assumes that the Exchange Server 2003 organization has a different default SMTP address space than the Exchange 5.5 organization, but that the users that have been migrated from the Exchange 5.5 organization need to use the Exchange 5.5 SMTP address space after migration.

Note   For information on configuring the sharing of SMTP address space in other scenarios see Knowledge Base article 822943: How to Share Simple Mail Transfer Protocol Address Spaces in Exchange 2003

1. In **Exchange System Manager**, expand **Recipients**, and then click **Recipient Policies** and select **New, Recipient Policy**.

2. Select **E-mail addresses** and then click **OK**. Type a name for the recipient policy. If you want to use this policy to assign the SMTP address to users in your organization, click **Modify** and configure the appropriate LDAP query.

3. Select the **E-Mail Addresses (Policy)** tab, click **New**, and then select **SMTP address** and click **OK**.

4. In the **Address** box, type the name of the shared SMTP address space using the @smtpdomainname format. Clear the check box for **This Exchange Organization is responsible for all mail delivery to this address**. Click **OK** twice.

The Exchange organization is now configured to be non-authoritative for the SMTP domain. To finish the configuration, you need to create an SMTP connector to route the mail for that domain to a specific host in the Exchange 5.5 organization. To do so, follow these steps:

1. In **Exchange System Manager**, expand the routing group where you want to configure the connector and right-click **Connectors**.

2. Select **New, SMTP Connector**.

3. Type a name for the connector.

4. Select **Forward all mail through this connector to the following smart hosts**, and then type the fully qualified domain name (FQDN) or the IP address of the server that e-mail for the shared SMTP address space is to be routed to. If you are using the IP address for the smart host, type this information inside brackets ([]).

5. Click **Add**, click a virtual server on the list to be a bridgehead, and then click **OK**.

6. On the **Address Space** tab, click **Add**, click **SMTP**, and then click **OK**.

7. In the **E-mail domain** box, type the SMTP address space without the (@) symbol. Click **OK**.

8. Because Exchange 2003 must receive messages for this domain also, click the **Allow messages to be relayed to these domains** check box. This setting makes it possible for all SMTP virtual servers that are listed as bridgeheads to accept messages for domain.

9. Click **OK**.

Verifying That a Server is Online

During troubleshooting, you may need to verify remotely that a server is online. This verification can include several steps. In most cases, you should start by verifying basic network connectivity, then verify name resolution, and then verify service availability.

1. To verify network connectivity, ping the IP address of the remote server. If the ping is successful, move on to the next step in troubleshooting. If the ping is not successful, determine whether there is a network failure by pinging another server in the same subnet, or by using **pathping** or **tracert** to determine where the failure occurs.

2. If the ping is successful, ping the fully qualified domain name of the server. If the ping is successful, move on to the next step. If the ping is not successful, use tools such as NSLookup or DNSLint to determine the DNS zone information and server configuration. You may also need to check the Hosts file; in most cases the Hosts file should not contain any information.

3. In some cases, clients may need to connect to the server using network basic input/output system (NetBIOS) names. This is true if you have older clients such as Microsoft Windows 95, Microsoft Windows 98, or Microsoft Windows NT® workstations on your network. To verify NetBIOS connectivity, use the **Net Use** command, or use Netdiag.exe. You can also use the **Browstat.exe** command (included in the Windows Server 2003 Support Tools) to perform detailed troubleshooting of NetBIOS browser troubleshooting.

4. If you can successfully connect to the server using host and NetBIOS names, the next step in troubleshooting is to test protocol connectivity. The best tool to test e-mail-related protocol connectivity is Telnet. If you cannot connect to the server using Telnet, verify that the required protocol is not blocked by a network device.

5. If you cannot connect to the server using Telnet, confirm that the required services are running on the Exchange server. The services that must be running on a front-end server are discussed in Securing a Front-End and Back-End Server Infrastructure in this Toolkit resource.

   The following services must be running on a back-end server:

   - Exchange System Attendant
   - Exchange store
   - Exchange System Manager
   - Windows Management Instrumentation
   - Microsoft Exchange Routing Engine
   - IIS Admin Service
   - SMTP
   - World Wide Web Publishing Service
   - Additional services, like NNTP, Exchange IMAP4, Exchange POP3, HTTP SSL Microsoft Exchange Event Service, Microsoft Exchange Site Replication Service, and Microsoft Exchange MTA Stacks, may be required to support Internet protocol clients or for compatibility with previous versions of Exchange.

Note These services are dependent on Windows Server 2003 services. View the properties of each service to confirm the service dependencies.

To verify the status of the services on a remote computer, you can connect to the computer using a custom Computer Management Microsoft Management Console (MMC) or Remote Desktop. If the required services are functional on the server, verify that the Exchange mailbox and public folder stores are mounted. You can use the Exchange System Manager to verify the mounted stores.

Notes

Notes

Notes

Notes

Notes

Notes